Daniel Cuonz, Scott Loren, Jörg Metelmann (eds.)
Screening Economies

Culture & Theory | Volume 183

Daniel Cuonz, Scott Loren, Jörg Metelmann (eds.)

Screening Economies

Money Matters and the Ethics of Representation

[transcript]

This research has been supported by

HANIEL
Stiftung

The European Haniel Program on Entrepreneurship and the Humanities

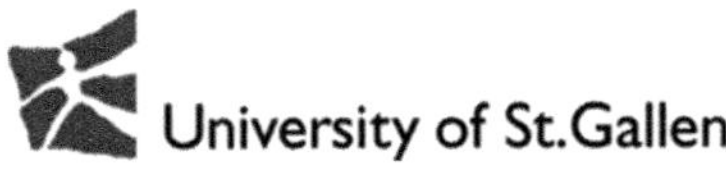

Research Panel Fund / Publication Fund

Bibliographic information published by the Deutsche Nationalbibliothek
The Deutsche Nationalbibliothek lists this publication in the Deutsche Nationalbibliografie; detailed bibliographic data are available in the Internet at http://dnb.d-nb.de

transcript Verlag | Hermannstraße 26 | D-33602 Bielefeld | live@transcript-verlag.de

Cover layout: Kordula Röckenhaus, Bielefeld
Cover illustration: Anthony Quintano (flickr.com), Fearless Girl Statue by Kristen Visbal (New York City Wall Street, CC BY 2.0)
Typeset by Francisco Bragança, Bielefeld
Printed by Majuskel Medienproduktion GmbH, Wetzlar
Print-ISBN 978-3-8376-4527-9
PDF-ISBN 978-3-8394-4527-3
https://doi.org/10.14361/9783839445273

Content

Lessons from "Fearless Girl"

Issues of Representation in Globalized Financial Capitalism

Daniel Cuonz, Scott Loren & Jörg Metelmann

Few places symbolize the financial economy's sovereignty of interpretation over social events in the atmospherically tangible manner of New York's Wall Street. Its most iconic figure is Arturo di Modica's famous *Charging Bull.* The impressive bronze statue (3.4 meters high, 5 meters long, and weighing 11 tons) appeared in New York's Financial District in 1989 as a response to the market crash two years earlier. According to its creator, its original purpose was to instill in its beholder a sense of strength and resilience with regard to the American economy. By the time of the Occupy movement it had come to symbolize something else for many: the arrogance, greed and recklessness of neoliberal finance capitalism. As prominently depicted in *Capitalism, A Love Story* (Michael Moore, 2009), *Charging Bull* had also taken on the symbolic weight of retroactively visualizing one of the most fatal speech acts uttered in the recent history of US-American economic policy. On March 28, 1985, president Ronald Reagan opened trading at the NYSE with a campaign-style speech to rally confidence in budget reform. Standing at his side was the president's chief of staff, former Merrill Lynch CEO Don Regan. With seconds to go before ringing in trading, the speech culminated with the now infamous claim, "We're gonna turn the bull loose."

And that is what happened. It seemed there was nothing left to keep neoliberal finance capitalism from running wild. Since then, the feral demeanor of the Bowling Green Bull increasingly represents uncontrollability in the eyes of many. Its high visibility and taint of arrogance have made it a spectacle in the most problematic sense of the word. Reduced to this limited range of meaning, it has also come to symbolize the system's lack of reasonable alternatives: something even high-ranking politicians and business representatives have repeatedly warned against, but to no avail. Who, then, could rein in this towering figure?

Since the spring of 2017, a new presence has lent this site of aesthetic impasse greater dynamism, even if by staging yet another figuration of impasse. Appearing on the Bowling Green during the night of March 7, Kristen Visbal's *Fearless Girl* faces the *Charging Bull* with an air of schoolgirl heroism: having watched the neighborhood bully abuse her friends one time too many, she takes the stance no one else could. Feet wide apart, hands on hips, *Fearless Girl* is vigorously defiant. Like her opponent, she symbolizes robust vitality and growth, but of a different kind. Her gesture of innocent obstinacy has the effect of both exceeding and halting her opponent. Juxtaposed to the *Charging Bull, Fearless Girl* embodies youth's uncorrupted and immovable sense of equitability.

Erected on the occasion of International Women's Day, the statue's purpose was to call attention to the inequitable representation of women in Russell 3000 index companies. Just as the statue's symbolic meaning has surpassed its early aspirations, the call to attention was successful beyond initial expectations. Democratic Senator Elizabeth Warren, a prominent voice in the fight against the power of the One Percent, was quick to post a selfie with the statue, adding the caption "Fight Like a Girl". The message was clear: everyone could be the Fearless Girl. The representation now stood not only for the limited number of women in high-ranking positions, though this remains central to the discourse. Manifested in the statue was now an additional imperative: to confront without trepidation Wall Street's belligerent urges for immediate satisfaction whatever the cost. Such inhumanity would no longer be tolerated.

Where *Charging Bull* has stood as a metaphor for unrestrained power localized in the hands of the few, and capable of bringing entire nations to the brink of collapse, *Fearless Girl* stands as a symbol for a more intelligent and humane society, one that will not succumb to economic brutality. *Fearless Girl*'s ability to break financial power's hold over iconic representation reassures us in our democratic convictions. In breaking the unholy alliance conjoining the financial economy and the attention economy, she makes the political potential of representation once again intelligible.

Redistribution of the Sensible

The fact that equitable representation cannot be taken for granted became immanently clear in the first moments of international financial crisis ten years ago, which continues to cast a long shadow over our lives. Large-scale financial crises differ from other forms of crisis with regard to a range of discrepancies. The number of people directly impacted on an existential level, and the quality of impact, are grossly disproportionate to the number of people directly involved and immediately responsible. The significantly smaller portion are people capable of understanding, and perhaps influencing, the state of things from the inside. Thus, the discrepancy in impact is also a discrepancy in intelligibility. While the financial economy's power over all other social figurations is only too palpable for many, its underlying mechanisms remain disastrously obscure. With every crash, when we approach the scene of spectacular misfortune, it is as if a representative of the law hails us with the halting message: *Move along. There's nothing to see here.* It is an uncomfortable half-truth. We know there is something to see; yet we recognize this as a site for the occlusion of meaning, not its production. This circumstance was aptly named "fiscal sublimity" (Vogl/Kluge 2009, 250; regarding the term's introduction, see Hamacher 1994, 172).

As the term elegantly expresses, the problem every criticism of contemporary capitalism faces is one of aesthetics. Kant identifies the limits of expression as a vital part of his aesthetics. He argues that any attempt to visualize the sublime by means of aesthetic expression is entirely unreasonable; arguing, however, that while "no sensible form can contain the sublime," the very fact of inadequacy "admits of sensible presentation" (Kant 2005, 62). Where the capacity for sensible representation reaches its limits, these limits can be made intelligible in their reflexive self-reference. To make the limits of expression intelligible is to sensibly incorporate the very fact of limit into processes of expression. Kant's foundational idea of philosophical aesthetics is more relevant than ever, but also more in need of renewal. For those interested in what critical representation might mean in the aftermath of the financial crisis, there is no getting around the question of how to give expression to that which resists clear articulation.

This question is a common denominator for all contributions collected in this volume. In their specificity, they provide a wide variety of approaches. What aesthetic means do we have to represent the economization of culture and society as they become concomitantly comprehensive and increasingly abstract? How can we constructively resist something whose effects we are painfully aware of, yet whose modes of functionality we do not quite understand? To ask how we can deal with such discrepancies is to consider how we have addressed them previously and how we might illustrate them presently. As such, questions as to the role of new media or the efficacy of contemporary art become relevant; particularly as sites for renegotiating the capacities of expression as they break from tradition.

With some inevitability, the challenge of expressing inexpressibility has moved to the center of reflections on economics in cultural and media studies. Regarding the cultural history of the monetary system, this is a rather intuitive move. The history is one of expanding "dematerialization" (Künzel 2011, 18); overwhelmingly under the management of smart machines and electric impulses, its hyperkinetic rate of expansion has finally made the great majority of systemic activity invisible. Since the emergence of "New Economic Criticism" (Woodmannsee/Osteen 1999, see also Cuonz 2018) in the 1980s, this topic had been approached from a variety of disciplinary perspectives. With its disciplinary roots in American cultural studies, and compelled by the political moment of Reagan-era neoliberalism, New Economic Criticism has tended to explore the dynamic intersections where literature, art and culture cross lines with economics, money and markets. The contingencies enabling Reagan-era neoliberalism at a specific historical moment had also necessitated a response from the field of cultural studies, whose business from the very beginning was a critical analysis of socio-cultural form as *per se* politico-aesthetic praxis. Where the contingencies of history had allowed state politics to dissociate economic and aesthetic claims to the social sovereignty of interpretation, the task of New Economic Criticism was to make visible their interdependence by exposing the manifold sites of imbrication. As a forerunner to current debates around questions of economic representation and representational economies, the pioneering work of Marc Shell and Jean-Joseph Goux has been essential to this undertaking.

Money and Representation

Shell's main contribution was to identify and illustrate homologies between forms in logic and literary writing and structures in the invention and function of money as a symbolic medium for economic trade

(Shell 1982, 3-4). While the appeal of such an approach to economy may be obvious from a cultural studies perspective, what it brings to the table is by no means negligible. If commercial and aesthetic economies can be shown to have developed from the same motives, that they are perhaps even connected by a "common anthropogenic root" (Woodmannsee & Osteen 1999, 15), then there is solid ground for aesthetic criticism to tackle the hegemony of economic forms in thought and expression. Screening the unfriendly take-over of non-economic forms in thought or expressive practices is no longer a matter of identifying economic patterns at work. It is a matter of counteracting the symptoms of their repressed common origin (cf. Shell 1982, 186-187). In "The Issue of Representation", Shell describes the monetary system's quasi-religious dependence on faith and trust accordingly: "Credit, or belief, involves the ground of aesthetic experience, and the same medium that confers belief in fiduciary money (bank notes) and in scriptural money (accounting records and money of account, created by the process of bookkeeping) also seems to confer it in art" (Shell 1999, 52).

Where Shell primarily engages in systematically demonstrating points of reference, Jean-Joseph Goux favors a historical approach to the homology between monetary and aesthetic representation:

> Was it purely by chance that the crisis of realism in the novel and in painting coincided with the end of gold money? Or that the birth of 'abstract' art coincided with the shocking invention of inconvertible monetary signs, now in general use? Can we not see in this double crisis of money and language the collapse of guarantees and frames of reference, a rupture between sign and thing, undermining representation and ushering in the age of the floating signifier? (Goux 1994, 3)

Goux's thesis gains traction when it takes the larger context of cultural theory into consideration, as evident in an even earlier work. In Symbolic Economies (1990 [1973]), he argues that the concept of general equivalence from Marxist value theory can be transferred to any area of culture in which symbolic exchange is governed by centralized hierarchical authority. He explains the abstract processes of determining value and importance as a reflexive negotiation between idealized general objects and particular objects. The idealized general object sets the parameters for value and importance while the particular object is subjected to these parameters.

Of particular interest is the capacity to recognize how concrete objects in a symbolic economy are dominated by an abstract general equivalent; and that this general equivalent occupies the structure-function position of an "empty, omnipotent center" (Goux 1990, 44). According to Goux, the establishment and consolidation of such symbolic monopolies take place throughout history in an ongoing "process of abstraction" (1990, 50). As a critical theory for reflection on monetary systems, the notion of progressive abstraction through symbolic monopoly has become relevant in ways unforeseeable from the perspective of its theoretical foundations.

In his 1999 essay "Cash, Check or Charge?", Goux made the condition of historicity clear in his reframing of the question every cashier had asked dozens and hundreds of times on a daily basis. At the time, he was able to described the process of increasing monetary abstraction with clairvoyant-like precision: "And what if this mutation of the sign and this mourning of representation were only the prelude to a still unknown ascendancy: the total bankerization of existence, by the combined powers of finance and computers?" (Goux 1999, 115). The accuracy of Goux's speculations about a future state of abstraction was all too clearly confirmed by the "fatal speculations" that led to the 2008 financial crisis. For Goux, there is no doubt that we are dealing with a "more general crisis" at the level "of basis (*fondement*) and foundation (*fondation*)" (Goux 2014, 219): a crisis in representation.

More explicitly than in his early works, Goux points to the need for an additional dimension of reflection on the relationship between money and representation in the aftermath of the sub-prime crisis. With new urgency, "not only the mechanisms that have ushered in catastrophe require inquiry" (Goux 2014, 204). He compels us to think more comprehensively about the fact that the manner in which economies had treated the term *value* over the years had thoroughly destroyed its foundations in reality and rational thought. As such, "it is not the economy alone that is affected; the entirety of (ethical and aesthetic) value has been banished by some radical 'frivolity'" (Goux 2014, 205).

Toward an Ethics of Representation

Goux' *J'accuse* might be rephrased as the call for an "ethics of representation". After all, the question of what *might* be shown inevitably raises another question: to what degree must that which is shown be exposed through an act of showing? "What is needed is a representational form whose native agency allows it to participate in an exchange while divesting it of accountability in the relativity of relations" (Hart Nibbrig 1994, 14). This desideratum served as the point of departure for this volume's investigation of economy aesthetics and informs all of its contributions. As such, the notion of economic *mediality* will play a vital role.

If cultural and media studies have been preoccupied with the concept of ownership for the analysis of media economies ("Who owns the media?"), the tendency in contemporary theory has been to examine mediality in economic systems. As Dommann, Hediger and Hoof (2018, 11) write: "this *economic turn* no longer understands economic processes as a secondary condition in the medial production of meaning, or as a field of application in film and media theory, but as a fundamental dimension whose specificity must be examined, and for which new interdisciplinary constellations and methods will be established accordingly."

The materiality of media processes continues to receive careful attention in this regard; from the establishment of communication infrastructures during the first and second industrial revolutions (Chandler 1977), to the transformative role of digital information and communication technologies in the third revolution (MacKenzie 2016). Brilliantly incorporated as the secret protagonist of Michael Lewis' *Flash Boys*, the competitive advantage of fiber optic cables in their relation to stock market tickers emphasizes how material practices of trade are media economies in a very pragmatic sense (*transfer, save, process*). An understanding of economies as medial forms is indispensible for a broader understanding of the economic. While cultural studies has been sensitized to this point from the beginning, the dynamics of media-economy continue to change.

Inscribing the recent present onto a distant past, Beyes and Pias have suggested that categories such as transparency, publicity and participation no longer apply to the new non-materiality of economic mediality, for which they propose the term *arcanum*. Unlike a secret, the *arcanum* cannot be revealed. It thus gestures to our present moment of formally inclusive nets and perceptually occluded work: "With the digitalization of further aspects of our lifeworld and with the countless number of apparatuses that can communicate with one another independently and can—the largest and smallest alike—control one another mutually and provide feedback to one another, these particularly cybernetic-temporal relations have more or less become absolute." (Beyes/Pias 2014, 114). Gumbrecht's "broad present" (Gumbrecht 2014) similarly addresses the inscrutable folds of contemporary hypermodernity. The mechanized feedback circuitry of cybernetic-temporal relations has collapsed the spaces of subjectivity, reflection and intention in its radical *perpetuum mobile* appropriation of the future. Concurring with Flusser that participation is "nonsense" (Beyes/Pias 2014, 114), Beyes and Pias recognize the incomprehensibility of high frequency trading as game-changing: while the future of market price development still provides the frame, it is the nanosecond of fiber-optic advantage that determines gains in the recent present. As the contemporary iteration of global capitalism, currents in flash-trade finance have displaced Smith's "invisible hand" – the secret of allocation of the "heart" in modern economic thought (Hediger 2014, 129) – with the *arcanum* of algorithms. If Beyes and Pias claim that it is structurally impossible to achieve transparency in the arcanum of algorithmic labor, perhaps this helps us to see the mythical quality of its former status: transparency as a waking dream of an unmediated world.

In recent years, the non-materiality of economic mediality has been lent form in its juxtaposition to narrative sense making, and inquiry into the epistemological conditions of economics. A volume edited by Peltzer, Lämmle and Wagenknecht (2012a) examines a variety of discursive forms (verbalizations, metaphors, agent knowledge, entertainment media) to illustrate how media representations of the financial crisis had transformed an incomprehensible phenomenon into a "communicable, socially shared reality" (2012b, 10), concluding that the medial capacity to make sense of the world, the material contours that mediate meaning, should thus be viewed critically. Parvulescu's 2017 volume on representations of financial crisis examines aesthetic forms specific to the hybrid medium of film still more closely; showing, amongst other things, how the cultural export of Hollywood cinema places the money flow *sub specie abstractionis* before the eyes of a worldwide audience.

Representing – Rethinking – Reframing

Reflecting distinctive currents in state-of-the-art thought and aesthetic praxes, the volume is divided into three conceptual categories.

Representing is concerned with novel modes of presentation in new media praxes in the wake of the vertical collapse of medium-specific technologies through digital convergence and the horizontal redistributions of production, circulation, consumption and remediation. Partial focus is placed on establishment media's reaction to new aesthetic and ideational dimensions of complexity and abstraction. This encompasses developments in televisual graphics and animations (Born), as well as cross-mapping narrative strategies in film (Metelmann). There is also a focus on medialities of distributive computing and blockchain security (Schnugg), as well as applications in social media data feeds and big data mining.

Rethinking is dedicated to the *aesthetic* and, by extension, *theoretical* implications of economic expression. Its contributions examine how literature and the arts might contribute to contemporary discourses in and on economic modernity. This includes critical reflections on financialization as a representational form *per se* alongside the art of representing financialization (Haiven). It provides counter-readings of technographic representation specific to the three conjunctural eras of reflexive modernity (Loren), and presents a comparative analysis of financial crisis and economic catastrophe as dramatized in the literary form of comedy (Cuonz). These contributions mobilize historical perspective in order to question the origins and original forms of rhetorical and dramatic performance. By identifying elements of economic and representational crisis, they explore the unconscious of aesthetic economies in of their economic depictions. Inquiry into the functionality of "financial fictions" leads to the realm of cultural sociology (Langenohl), with its system-theoretical perspectives (system theory, subjectivation).

Reframing provides a stage for actors specialized in making the occult aspects of the financial system visible for all. In the spirit of interventionist ethnography, the sociologist Aeron Davis takes a top-down vertical perspective on the financial crisis in more than three hundred interviews with high-profile corporate staff from Britain's private and public financial industry. Against this backdrop, he advocates use of the term *financialization* as a new conceptual orientation for critical discourse on capitalism. New York-based artist and celebrated "hacktivist" Paolo Cirio intervenes in the flows of digital-network capitalism and maps novel spaces of resistance with his conceptual, schematic and participatory art. Imanuel Schipper, a dramatist of the popular German-Swiss collective "Rimini Protokoll", rearranges key scenes of contemporary economic convention (shareholder meetings, the World Economic Forum) with the tools of advanced post-dramatic theater.

As opposed to constituting a conclusion, the third section employs a strategy of opening possible perspectives. It exemplifies what the volume as a whole aims to achieve: an open exchange involving both academic and non-academic debates, from both theoretical and interventional perspectives. What is at stake, after all, is not only the matter of reflection on aesthetic possibility; it is a matter of aesthetic engagement as a possible political form. To recall again *Fearless Girl* – and her symbolic courage in standing up to the belligerent character of speculative finance – resistance is a *resist-stance.* If Wall Street symbolizes the sovereignty of finance, it also recalls to us sovereign power's capacity to resist representation and its tendency to generate sites of aesthetic impasse. The vitality and strength represented in *Fearless Girl* are a powerful reminder to us all of the vital role representation plays in bringing about real change.

* * *

We would like to thank the University of St. Gallen's Grundlagenforschungsfonds and Publikationsfonds for their generous support of the October 2017 conference "Screening Economies" and of this publication. We would also like to express our gratitude to the Haniel Stiftung in Duisburg for their further support through the "European Haniel Program on Entrepreneurship and the Humanities". The enriching collegial exchange at the conference sessions in St. Gallen and at the Kunsthaus Bregenz would not have been possible without Sabrina Helmer's organizational assistance. We are also grateful to Thomas D. Trummer for his generous invitation to join him on the other side of the lake for the second day of the conference. Last but not least, thank you to David Matley and Patrick Ploschnitzki, who contributed in the editing and translation of texts.

English translation: Patrick Ploschnitzki[1]

1 | The translation has been reworked by the authors, quotes have been translated by Daniel Cuonz (French) and Scott Loren (German).

References

Beyes, Timon/Pias, Claus (2014): Transparenz und Geheimnis: *ZfK – Zeitschrift für Kulturwissenschaften* 8, no. 2, 111-17.

Chandler, Alfred D. (1977): *The Visible Hand. The Managerial Revolution in American Business.* Cambridge, MA: Harvard University Press.

Cuonz, Daniel (2019): New Economic Criticism. In: Vogl, Joseph/Burkhard, Wolf (eds.): *Handbuch Literatur und Ökonomie.* Berlin/New York: De Gruyter [forthcoming].

Dommann, Monika/Hediger, Vinzenz/Hoof, Florian (2018): Medienökonomien. Einleitung in den Schwerpunkt. *Zeitschrift für Medienwissenschaft* 18, no. 1, 10-17.

Goux, Jean-Joseph (1990 [1973]): *Symbolic Economies. After Marx and Freud.* Trans. Jennifer Curtis Gage, Ithaca, NY: Cornell University Press.

Goux, Jean-Joseph (1994 [1984]): *The Coiners of Language.* Norman, OK: University of Oklahoma Press.

Goux, Jean-Joseph (1999): Cash, Check or Charge? The New Economic Criticism. Studies at the Intersection of Literature and Economics. In: Woodmannsee, Martha/Osteen, Mark (eds.): *The New Economic Criticism. Studies at the Intersection of Literature and Economics.* London/New York: Routledge, 114-27.

Goux, Jean-Joseph (2014): Speculations fatales [2008]. In: Goux, Jean-Joseph: Id.: *Fractures du temps.* Paris, 203-220.

Gumbrecht, Hans-Ulrich (2014): *Our Broad Present. Time and Contemporary Culture.* New York: Columbia University Press.

Hamacher, Werner (1994): Faust, Geld. *Athenäum. Jahrbuch für Romantik* 4, 131-187.

Hart Nibbrig, Christiaan Lucas (1994): Zum Drum und Dran einer Fragestellung. Ein Vorgeschmack. In: Hart Nibbrig, Christiaan Lucas (ed.): *Was heißt "Darstellen"?* Frankfurt (Main): Suhrkamp, 7-14.

Hediger, Vinzenz (2014): Technik, Trieb, Markt, Leben. Vom Nachleben des Arkanums in der Moderne. Eine Replik auf Beyes/Pias. *ZfK – Zeitschrift für Kulturwissenschaften,* no. 2, 126-30.

Kant, Immanuel (2005 [1790]): *Critique of Judgment.* Trans. J. H. Bernard. Mineola, NY: Dover Publications.

Künzel, Christine (2011): Finanzen und Fiktionen. Eine Einleitung. In: Künzel, Christine/Hempel, Dirk (eds.): *Finanzen und Fiktionen.*

Grenzgänge zwischen Literatur und Wirtschaft, Frankfurt (Main): Campus Verlag, 9-24.

Lewis, Michael (2014): *Flash Boys: A Wall Street Revolt*. New York: Norton & Company.

MacKenzie, Donald (2016): Capital's Geodesic. Chicago, New Jersey, and the Material Sociology of Speed. In: Wajcman, Judy/Dodd, Nigel (eds.): *The Sociology of Speed: Digital, Organizational, and Social Temporalities*. Oxford: Oxford University Press, 55-71.

Parvulescu, Constantin (ed.) (2017): *Global Finance on Screen: From Wall Street to Side Street*. London/New York: Routledge.

Peltzer, Anja/Lämmle, Kathrin/Wagenknecht, Andreas (eds.) (2012a): *Krise, Cash & Kommunikation – Analysen zur Darstellung der Finanzkrise in den Medien*. Konstanz: UVK.

Peltzer, Anja/Lämmle, Kathrin/Wagenknecht, Andreas (2012b): Die Finanzkrise in den Medien, eine Einleitung. In: Peltzer, Anja/Lämmle, Kathrin/Wagenknecht, Andreas (eds.) (2012a): *Krise, Cash & Kommunikation – Analysen zur Darstellung der Finanzkrise in den Medien*. Konstanz: UVK, 9-20.

Shell, Marc (1982): *Money, Language and Thought. Literary and Philosophic Economies from the Medieval to the Modern Era*. Berkeley, CA: University of California Press.

Shell, Marc (1999): The Issue of Representation. In: Woodmannsee, Martha/Osteen, Mark (eds.): *The New Economic Criticism. Studies at the Intersection of Literature and Economics*. London/New York: Routledge, 114-27.

Vogl, Joseph/Kluge, Alexander (2009): *Soll und Haben. Fernsehgespräche*. Zurich: Diaphanes.

Woodmannsee, Martha/Osteen, Mark (1999): Taking Account of the New Economic Criticism. An Historical Introduction. In: Woodmannsee, Martha/Osteen, Mark (eds.): *The New Economic Criticism. Studies at the Intersection of Literature and Economics*. London/New York: Routledge, 3-50.

How to Measure the Economy Using Big Data

Agustín Indaco

According to many economists, practically every decision in life is an economic decision. It is easy to see how deciding whether to buy the more expensive butter or the cheaper margarine at the grocery store is an economic decision. But economists tend to believe that who we decide to marry, whether to commit a crime or not or even how the organ donor market should be regulated are all governed by the same economic principles one is taught in an introductory economics course (Becker 1974a, b; Roth et al. 2003). I will not try to argue in favor or against this in this chapter. Rather, let's take this premise as true at face value for now, and see how economics should be studied nowadays under this light.

Economists tend to study the economy through data. Different economic measures allow them to see, among other things, whether the economy is functioning well, the rate at which prices are increasing and how many people are unemployed. In the same way that doctors use MRI scans and X-rays to diagnose patients, economists have their own set of economic measures to diagnose the state of the economy. The problem is that just as the human body is made up of millions of cells (actually trillions), the economy is made up of millions of individuals. No two individuals are the same or behave identically. Thus, using aggregate measures or overall averages to understand how individuals function within an economy is as vague as if doctors only cared about the general status of your health when trying to identify a tumor. Luckily today, Big Data provides novel data sources that allow us to study the intricacies and details behind many socio-economic issues. We can now go into much more detail than the *average* and study human decisions and economic outcomes for individuals facing different realities, which allows for a much more precise representation of the economy.

But economists have been slow in adopting these technologies in their research. Although there has been a well-established data revolution in the last 60 years in papers published in top economic journals (Hamermesh 2012), the field has not yet completely adopted these novel data sources. The bulk of empirical economic research is still done using small-sample government surveys. These datasets have been the status quo in academia. Given that these surveys are conducted specifically for policymakers and researchers to study and monitor the economy, it is easy to extract conventional indicators about the economy from them. However, they are designed to be nationally representative, i.e. to understand how the average citizen lives, works and goes through her daily activities. But the differences between how individuals live and work are vast, so understanding how the average person lives provides little information to estimate the effect a policy has on each individual. The Big Data available today lets us take a quantum leap in this regard.

Increasingly, our everyday life and the decisions we make are being captured and stored in the ongoing dataset that is our digital footprint. The decision process we go through to buy a book on the internet can be traced by our search history. The commuting route and medium we take to work is tracked by our mobile phones. The physical activity we engage in each day and the amount and quality of sleep we get is captured by smart watches and health apps. Every day, billions of people around the world decide to share and represent their daily lives through social media. Companies and for-profit enterprises have radically changed the way they operate; not only as an active feedback loop of how their products and services are being evaluated, but also to more precisely target potential consumers. In fact, they are already actively tapping into this information to perfect their modes of operation. Unfortunately, the use of this data in more socially beneficial domains has lagged behind. Although there are several projects that have incorporated Big Data sources, which I will outline in this chapter, this has yet to revolutionize the field. This trove of information is being seriously neglected by economists.

By means of Big Data, economists can bridge the gap between the outcomes of their tedious economic models and people's real decisions and everyday lives. The data is there, people are increasingly giving (willingly or unwillingly) researchers the opportunity to study in detail what they do. The data revolution is a panacea for the economics profession at a time when it is in dire need of a radical change. Economists should really take advantage of this opportunity.

Throughout this chapter I will present several examples of studies that have used various novel data sources to study economic decisions by individuals. Some of these endeavors have allowed scholars to answer questions that were previously unfathomable, given the complexity or the guarded nature of some of the issues. Others have allowed us to uncover a new layer of the intricate socio-economic realities faced today.

An important issue to address at this time is that of the representativeness of these data sources. There are two distinctively important issues surrounding this issue which should not be taken lightly when using these data sources for research purposes, as they can lead to biased and incorrect assertions about society, people's lives and decision-making. Even though the number of observations can be overwhelmingly large (in the realm of trillions), we never truly have *all* the observations. Not everyone uses digital payment methods or the internet to buy books and not everyone has social media accounts. Not recognizing these limitations can lead to dangerously erroneous understandings of socio-economic behavior. There are large segments of society that are vastly underrepresented in 'Big Data' datasets. For example, the Visual Earth project[1] analyzed the growth of image sharing on Twitter around the world, and found that even though image sharing in developing countries was growing at a faster pace than that in developed countries, the overall percentage of images posted from developing countries was much smaller than their percentage of the world population. A second issue to consider, and maybe more specific to each data source itself, is that even when people are registered in certain services, they may self-select when to use them and what to show. In this sense, credit card transactions are probably not an ideal source to study consumption of illegal goods or services. Similarly, what users choose to post on social media is probably a skewed representation of their daily activities.

Although, due to the scope of this chapter, I will not be developing these issues extensively, it is crucial to bear in mind both of these factors when conducting this type of research as well as when assessing the quality of research projects that use Big Data sources.

1 | http://visual-earth.net/

Measuring the Impossible

There are several advantages for economists and other social researchers in using Big Data. Several papers have exploited the high frequency of these datasets to estimate economic variables at higher frequencies than traditionally available (Choi and Varian 2012; Ginsberg et al. 2009). Other papers have used the geographical granularity of the data to estimate regional poverty measures in Africa at the subnational level, figures which are not available from official statistics offices (Blumenstock et al. 2015). Although these are extremely valuable characteristics that expand the frontier of the type of questions that may be answered by economists, I will concentrate here on a different attribute of these data sources.

Traditional empirical research in economics is based on survey data, either collected by official government agencies or by researchers themselves. But what individuals reveal when responding to survey questionnaires is not always accurate (Tourangeau et al. 2000). Consciously or unconsciously, people tend to under- or overestimate certain attributes in their lives or choose not to disclose certain information they deem private. But even more interestingly, there are only certain aspects of economic thinking that can be parsed out of surveys. Even if one wanted to reveal this information, who knows how many books one browsed before deciding to buy this one? Can anyone really recall how many times one went to a certain restaurant in the last year? And how long they stayed there during each visit? And where they were before and after? All of this information is already being captured by different devices many of us frequently interact with or carry around in our daily lives. In this sense, these alternative data sources reveal information that is difficult, or sometimes impossible, to capture using traditional survey data. Using these datasets has the potential to understand the intricate realities and details of people's economic activities and lives. Furthermore, given the large number of observations in these novel datasets, one is able to study behavior at an acutely detailed level. They have the capacity to go beyond the aggregate level measurements of consumption and income that are used by economists today to measure economic outcomes and realities.

Perhaps one of the best cases to date of the use of Big Data in economics is the research done by Raj Chetty and his team of researchers, which they have collectively labeled The Equality of Opportunity Project. The Internal Revenue Service (IRS) gave them access to the tax records of all Americans between 1996 and 2012, initially with the intent to study the effects of taxation policy. But the team of researchers found few interesting results on this front: they were mostly replicating, albeit more precisely, results from previous work done using survey data. So they aborted that path and started thinking of other possible uses for the dataset. They realized that the salient novelty of this dataset was that they had so many observations, which allowed them to see important patterns at the neighborhood level. This is something that cannot be done with traditional survey datasets, given that they have at most only a handful of observations from some neighborhoods.

Raj Chetty and his team started looking into social mobility patterns: What are the chances that children born into low-income families become high-income earners themselves? For this they focused on all children born in the U.S. between 1980 and 1982 and measured their income in 2011-12, when they were approximately 30 years old. They found substantial variation in social mobility across areas: while some cities had mobility rates comparable to countries with the highest mobility (e.g. Denmark), other cities had mobility rates lower than any other developed country in the world.

But it still was not clear if neighborhoods had a causal effect on upward mobility or if the differences between geographic areas was due to systematic differences in the characteristics of the residents living in each area. To answer this, the researchers focused on families who moved from a city with low mobility rates to a city with high mobility rates. By analyzing the share of the difference in income between these two cities that a child obtains by moving at different ages, they were able to calculate the exposure effect, i.e. how much of the neighborhood effect was being captured by children in their future earnings. They found that relative to those who moved at younger ages, children who moved at later ages had steadily declining incomes. The effect completely disappeared at age 23, after which no gain was achieved by moving. Interestingly, the authors found an equal and opposite effect for children whose families moved to worse areas. This sort of fine-grained policy analysis, which is not possible with survey data, has the possibility of radically changing how we understand the economy and thus implement policies that provide opportunities for families to succeed. For example, this shows that much of a person's income prospects is set before they enter the labor market.

Social media content is another generator of data at the disposal of researchers today that gives an insight into social factors. These data sources allow researchers to study what people care about or pay attention to at any moment in time, detect urban mobility patterns and study social networks. First of all, social media analysis has given researchers an unprecedented in-depth look at social interactions and social networks.[2] Previous theoretical, experimental and quasi-experimental work has found that if there is information about a job vacancy within a network, then the job finding prospects of all network members improve on average (Beaman and Magruder 2012; Calvó-Armengol and Jackson 2004). But even though these papers find that there is an average improvement, little is known about which network members benefit the most.

A person's social network is made up of ties with varying tie strength (e.g. a close friend is a stronger tie and an acquaintance is a weaker tie). If social ties of differing strength benefit more, then this may result in the allocation of a job away from one person and toward another with the right type of connection (weak or strong), but who might not be necessarily a better worker. One popular notion based on Granovetter's (1973) theoretical model was that for finding jobs, weak ties were more valuable than strong ties, since strong ties have redundant information, while weak ties hold new information. Much of the previous empirical work has been limited by the scope of the available data. Many studies use self-reported tie strength that may suffer biases, be firm-specific or only have information for a subset of a person's full network. This is one such example where social media platforms fill the void of information. Using data on 6 million Facebook users, Gee et al. (2017) found that while it is true that the majority of job seekers find work through their weak ties, a person is more likely to obtain a job if the information comes from a strong tie relative to a weak tie. The first result derives from the fact that a majority of our connections are weak, and thus the overall probability that we end up finding work through a weak link is larger.

Social media also allow us to take a deep look into which topics are of interest to people in different income groups. Preoţiuc-Pietro et al. (2015) collected tweets posted by people with associated job titles and mapped

2 | To validate and contextualize this research, it is important to understand that studies have found that online communities are very similar to offline networks in their structure and size (Mayer 2009; Pollet et al. 2011; Gonçalves et al. 2011).

this information onto the median income for each industry. By doing so they created a rich dataset of more than 10 million tweets from people in different occupations. Not only were they able to find well-known patterns between demographic characteristics and income (e.g. on average men earn more than women, African Americans earn less than Caucasians and income increases with education level), but they were also able to study the content of tweets and see how it relates to users' income. Using language processing techniques, they found that neutral sentiment in tweets increases with income, while both positive and negative sentiment decreases. High income users tend to talk about politics or corporate issues on social media, not personal matters. In contrast, lower income users tend to voice more subjectivity online, expressing more emotions, such as sadness, disgust and surprise. They tend to talk about relationships and use emotive language, both positive and negative.

Studying Inequality

Inequality has been widely researched by economists and social scientists. During the 20th century, different measures were developed to capture the statistical dispersion of income or wealth. But these statistics do not provide the whole story. They are extremely powerful and useful in summarizing a very complicated phenomenon into one number that can be compared across geographical regions, but they do not provide context on how individuals living in one extreme or the other of the income curve live.

The project "On Broadway"[3] gives a glimpse of these realities by creating an interactive map from images and socio-economic data of the emblematic Broadway street through Manhattan. Dividing Broadway into 30-meter long segments, the researchers combined data and images taken along Broadway from Instagram, Twitter, Foursquare, Google Street View, taxi rides and select U.S. Census indicators. The resulting map consists of many layers of images and information that represents the urban structure and activities carried out along this iconic thoroughfare. A quick glance at this map shows the stark income inequality that exists between the southern and northern sections of Broadway. Furthermore, a positive correlation is found between the median income and the number of

3 | http://www.on-broadway.nyc/

social media posts from the different sources in each of these segments: in affluent areas, people post more photos on social media, 'check in' to more locations on Foursquare and take more taxis; and vice versa. Beyond the ultimate measures that replicate inequality in a different manner, this project allows us to study more nuanced differences in each location. As one moves along Broadway using the interactive map, one can analyze how the building's façade, color pallets and even content shared on social media differ as one moves from more affluent areas to less affluent zones.

A closer insight into these differences was provided by Indaco and Manovich (2016), who combined 7.5 million Instagram images posted from New York between March and August 2014 with census data to explore the relationship between the distribution of income and Instagram images across Census tracts. The visual-centric format of Instagram creates a distinct image for different parts of a city, which allows for quantitative and qualitative comparison of spatial patterns. Several interesting results emerge that could not have been captured with traditional economic analysis and tools. Using the dates of shared images to estimate whether a particular user lives in NY or is only visiting, the sample of users is divided between locals and tourists. The sharing patterns and distribution of these two groups differ considerably. Tourists' image sharing is highly concentrated in a few areas with well-known attractions, such as Times Square and the Empire State Building. In fact, more than 50 percent of images taken by tourists are from areas that represent 12 percent of the city. While the distribution of images by neighborhood does change from more touristic areas to more night-life locations as the day progresses, there is no difference between weekday and weekend patterns. For locals, the distribution of images is more evenly distributed throughout the city, but there are distinct patterns that mimic the commuting patterns of the residents. During working hours, the distribution of images is concentrated largely in business areas, whereas during night-time they spread more evenly across the city. For locals, there are also large differences between the patterns that emerge during weekdays relative to weekends, with the latter being more disperse.

But it is possible to conduct an even more detailed study: by analyzing the time, frequency and location from where posts are shared we can infer the Census tracts where users live. By merging this with Census data, we can obtain socio-economic characteristics of households in each area. This gives us an idea of the places that individuals from different socio-economic groups frequent during the day and what they choose to share, and allows us to live through their eyes (or at least through what they wish to show). One interesting figure emerging from this is that roughly 73 percent of images posted by residents living in less affluent neighborhoods (with median incomes below $40,000) are taken in more affluent neighborhoods (with incomes above $100,000). Conversely, only 12 percent of images taken by residents from more affluent neighborhoods are from less affluent neighborhoods. Considering Jane Jacobs' claim that what makes cities special is that they spark random interactions between their citizens (Jacobs, 1992), this sheds light on where these interactions might take place, and what that means for city life and social mobility. This sort of analysis allows policy makers and urban developers to understand how a city works and how individuals from different income sectors might interact.

Beyond the detailed scope of the data now available, these novel datasets also allow us to study sensitive issues that individuals may not wish to disclose in surveys. Stephens-Davidowitz (2013) showcases a range of such issues. The author uses data on the swarm of Google searches conducted by individuals to parse out what people really think and do regarding sensitive issues they are likely not to disclose publicly. For example, several studies based on reported child maltreatment rates concluded that child abuse cases had not increased during the Great Recession in the U.S. in 2008-09 (Lindo et al. 2013). In fact, studies from previous economic downturns had even found that poor economic conditions were associated with a decline in child abuse cases (Paxson and Waldfogel 1999). Using Google search data on phrases such as "child abuse" or "child neglect", Stephens-Davidowitz (2013) found an increase in maltreatment in recession-hit communities: a one percentage point increase in the unemployment rate increases maltreatment by roughly 2.5 percent. Further research found that, as state budgets are slashed during times of recession, which negatively impacts the services provided by child abuse prevention agencies, this leads to long waits on child abuse hotlines and many individuals hang up before their call is taken. This explains why previous studies had found lower rates during recessions when studying the issue using officially reported data.

Conclusion

If, as economists believe, economics is involved in every decision we make in our daily lives, then the scope of work and knowledge that currently stems from economic research is quite underwhelming. Given that technological advancements have changed how we perform many daily activities, from interacting with friends to buying groceries, allowing us to track many of these decisions and interactions, the use of novel data sources should be central to how we study the economy and society. This data can be used for the benefit of society and public policy, not only by private companies to fine-tune their advertising. This needs to be the groundbreaking revolution that changes the way economics is studied.

Economists diagnose and understand the economy through data. Nowadays, individuals broadcast and share (consciously or not) a large part of their daily activities. If the data that economists use to study the economy is only representative of the average individual, then it is hard for the field to develop ideas that truly represent individuals in their different realities. Datasets that would allow this did not exist previously. But for the first time in history, this data is increasingly available. Economists should take advantage of this opportunity to revolutionize economic research.

References

Beaman, Lori/Jeremy Magruder (2012): Who Gets the Job Referral? Evidence from a Social Networks Experiment. *American Economic Review* 102, no. 7, 3574-93.

Becker, Gary (1974a): A Theory of Marriage. NBER Chapters: National Bureau of Economic Research, Inc, 1974. https://econpapers.repec.org/bookchap/nbrnberch/2970.htm.

Becker, Gary (1974b): Crime and Punishment: An Economic Approach. NBER Chapters: National Bureau of Economic Research, Inc, 1974. https://econpapers.repec.org/bookchap/nbrnberch/3625.htm.

Blumenstock, Joshua/Cadamuro, Gabriel/On, Robert (2015): Predicting Poverty and Wealth from Mobile Phone Metadata. *Science* 350, no. 6264, 1073-76.

Calvó-Armengol, Antoni/Jackson, Matthew O. (2004): The Effects of Social Networks on Employment and Inequality. *American Economic Review* 94, no. 3, 426-54.

Chetty, Raj/Hendren, Nathaniel (2016): The Impacts of Neighborhoods on Intergenerational Mobility II: County-Level Estimates. NBER Working Paper. National Bureau of Economic Research, Inc. https://econpapers.repec.org/paper/nbrnberwo/23002.htm.

Choi, Hyunyoung/Varian, Hal (2012): Predicting the Present with Google Trends. *The Economic Record* 88, no. 1, 2-9.

Gee, Laura K./Jones, Jason/Burke, Moira (2017): Social Networks and Labor Markets: How Strong Ties Relate to Job Finding on Facebook's Social Network. *Journal of Labor Economics* 35, no. 2, 485-518.

Ginsberg, Jeremy/Mohebbi, Matthew H./Patel, Rajan S./Brammer, Lynnette/Smolinski, Mark S./Brilliant, Larry (2009): Detecting Influenza Epidemics Using Search Engine Query Data. *Nature* 457, no. 7232, 1012-14.

Gonçalves, Bruno/Perra, Nicola/Vespignani, Alessandro (2011): Modeling Users' Activity on Twitter Networks: Validation of Dunbar's Number. *PLoS ONE* 6, no. 8, e22656.

Granovetter, Mark S. (1973): The Strength of Weak Ties. *American Journal of Sociology* 78, no. 6, 1360-80.

Hamermesh, Daniel (2012): Six Decades of Top Economics Publishing: Who and How? NBER Working Paper. National Bureau of Economic Research, Inc. https://econpapers.repec.org/paper/nbrnberwo/18635.htm.

Indaco, Agustín/Manovich, Lev (2016): Urban Social Media Inequality: Definition, Measurements, and Application. *ArXiv:1607.01845 [Physics]*. http://arxiv.org/abs/1607.01845.

Jacobs, Jane (1992): *The Death and Life of Great American Cities*. New York: Vintage Books.

Lindo, Jason/Schaller, Jessamyn/Hansen, Benjamin (2013): Economic Conditions and Child Abuse. IZA Discussion Paper. Institute for the Study of Labor (IZA). https://econpapers.repec.org/paper/izaizadps/dp7355.htm.

Mayer, Adalbert (2009): Online Social Networks in Economics. *Decision Support Systems*, Online Communities and Social Network, 47, no. 3, 169-84.

Paxson, Christina/Waldfogel, Jane (1999): Parental Resources and Child Abuse and Neglect. *American Economic Review* 89, no. 2, 239-44.

Pollet, Thomas V./Roberts, Sam G.B./Dunbar, Robin I.M. (2011): Use of Social Network Sites and Instant Messaging Does Not Lead to

Increased Offline Social Network Size, or to Emotionally Closer Relationships with Offline Network Members. *Cyberpsychology, Behavior, and Social Networking* 14, no. 4, 253-58.

Preoţiuc-Pietro, Daniel/Volkova, Svitlana/Lampos, Vasileos/Bachrach, Yoram/Aletras, Nikolaos (2015): Studying User Income through Language, Behaviour and Affect in Social Media. *PLoS ONE* 10, no. 9, e0138717.

Roth, Alvin E./Sonmez, Tayfun/Ünver, M. Utku (2003): Kidney Exchange. Working Paper. NBER Working Paper: National Bureau of Economic Research, Inc.

Stephens-Davidowitz, Seth Isaac (2013): Essays Using Google Data. https://dash.harvard.edu/handle/1/10984881.

Tourangeau, Roger/Rips, Lance J./Rasinski, Kenneth (2000): *The Psychology of Survey Response*. Cambridge: Cambridge University Press.

Blockchain and *Bodies© INCorporated*

Media Arts Screening Economic Innovation 2.0

Claudia Schnugg

In society, culture and philosophy, many functions have been ascribed to the arts throughout the centuries: from their communicational function regarding the state of the art in society and culture to their creative capacities (Belfiore/Bennett 2006). Since modernity, the arts, and especially since the 1960s the emerging media arts, positioned themselves at the forefront of newness and innovation. Media arts not only have the reputation of being at the forefront of technological and scientific development, but from the very beginning of the exploration of kinetics, the early computer arts, the inclusion of newest technologies, hardware and software, also created a dialog between artists, scientists and engineers working in that field. In this dialog, artists and artistic exploration of technologies allowed fields such as computer visualization and computer graphics to emerge as an independent field within computer science (Taylor 2014).

However, media arts and the artistic exploration of scientific fields did not stop at the invention of new technologies in mid-20th century. Parallel to the development of the newest scientific disciplines and cutting-edge research in scientific fields, artists entered into these fields and worked on questions related to the science being done. They started to actively engage in dialog and collaborate with scientists, raised ethical and critical questions about ideas and processes, spun ideas in science fiction and speculative design processes, communicated outcomes and scientific opportunities through their artwork and enabled public engagement in the scientific process through their activities (Bureaud 2018, Dumitriu 2018). In these projects, artists such as Oron Catts, Victoria Vesna and Anna Dumitriu demonstrated how they can create important artworks that push the boundaries of scientific disciplines and public engagement: Oron Catts and Ionat Zurr made visionary statements on the artificial production of leather and meat with *The Tissue Culture & Art* (2001); Victoria Vesna and nanoscientist James Gimzewski examined the metamorphoses of butterflies through sonification in *Blue Morph* (2007); and Anna Dumitriu, with her scientific partners Sarah Goldberg, Rob Neely and Heather Macklyne in her *Make do and Mend* project entitled *Controlled Commodity* (2018), explored the development of antibiotic resistance, its cultural embeddedness and modern technologies such as gene-editing via CRISPR.

The visionary statements artists make in these collaborative projects at the interface of art and science push the boundaries of the disciplines, but also help to reach out to broader society. They make scientific visions and experiments accessible by contextualization of the work being done in an environment that is understandable by a broader public, but also reflects the broader social value of the scientific work being done back to scientists, who often merely focus on the necessities within the scientific community that allow for scientific contribution and publication. But art can do more than showing and visualizing scientific outcomes, economic innovations or social trends. It can make the main ideas and visions experiential, can subvert and reconfigure ideas observed through critical approaches, and by extension, a broader public is allowed to participate in ushering in new paradigms.

And with these opportunities, artists do not only approach scientific work and the latest technologies, they also reflect on societal issues and screen economic developments. A case that is closely connected to computer science, the application of cutting-edge technologies, societal changes and economics is blockchain. Blockchain is something very intangible as it differs very much from everything we know in society and culture, and it addresses societal and economic change that is decoupled from the predominant economic and business logics that constitute large parts of societies and governmental approaches. Scientists, technologists, economists and sociologists struggle to provide an explanation for blockchain's technical foundations, its central functionality and the societal changes its introduction could trigger.

Media artists started to explore blockchain, the opportunities it provides and the social implications it can bring (Catlow et al. 2017). Most of the recently developed artwork in this field mainly focuses on the technical functionalities of blockchain, such as *Lightcoin* (2017), a media art piece by Hrvoje Hiršl. The artwork plays with the physical phenomena of particle entanglement, the physical limitations by the speed of light of current cryptosystems and a website platform that monitors market fluctuations and provides informative texts. Important as such artworks are for communicating the development of cryptosystems based on blockchain mechanisms, and as essential such artistic interpretation is in awareness building and public education, they tend to lean towards explanation of the system instead of experiencing the system's implications.

The recently re-invented art project *Bodies© INCorporated* (also called *Bodies© Inc* in its original version, *Bodies Inc 2.0* in the recent version; both can be referred to as *Bodies© INCorporated* as one body of art work) by Victoria Vesna tackles this missing aspect of experiential access to blockchain, its social implications and changed economies based on cryptosystems. The artwork itself already has a long history of displaying economic and social developments through technological innovation, as in the original version of *Bodies© Inc* that was initiated by Victoria Vesna in the early 1990s. The recent iteration of the project uses the basic idea and initially created environment of this early net art piece to explore the potentials of blockchain in the world of *Bodies© Inc.* The ongoing development of the new version of *Bodies Inc 2.0* overlaps with a revived interest in the original art project, as it was selected for the web art/net art archive *Net Anthology* by Rhizome in spring 2017. On the following pages, I will dive into the world of *Bodies Inc 2.0* and follow its development throughout nearly three decades to learn about the intensity of such participatory and interactive artworks in the communication of complex issues and implications of abstract technologies for society, especially through economic developments.

Fig. 1: Bodies© INCorporated *by Victoria Vesna, main page of the original version, Screenshot of the current online representation by Claudia Schnugg (http://www.bodiesinc.ucla.edu/frames1.html).*

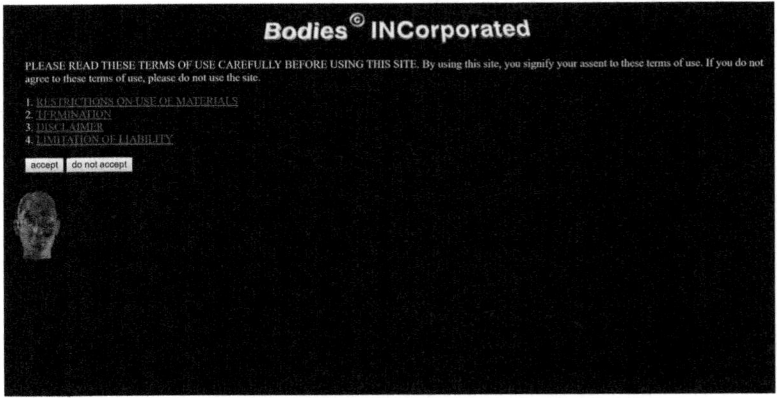

Fig. 2: Bodies Inc 2.0 *by Victoria Vesna, main page of the updated version, 3D design by Sanglim Han, Screenshot of the current online representation by Claudia Schnugg (www.bodiesinc.com).*

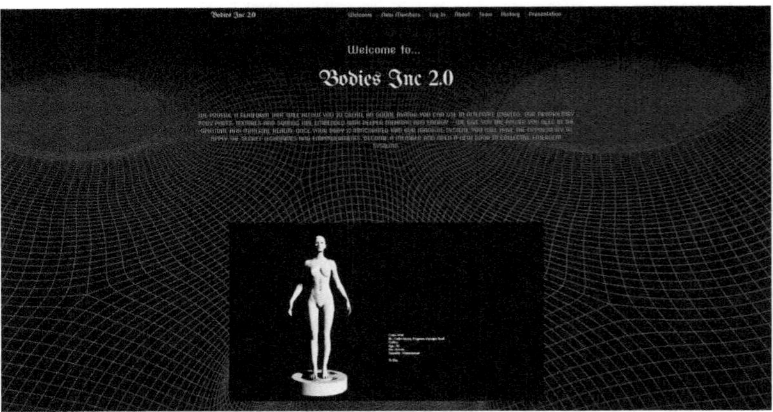

After some initial experimentation with the idea of a net art piece, in 1993 Victoria Vesna started the project to develop *Bodies© Inc* as an interactive experiential artwork, which first took shape in 1996 as one of the first 3D net art pieces worldwide. As such it has been extensively presented and reflected upon. From the very beginning, the project focused on the display of how new developments could be integrated into the existing art market and established gallery system. At the same time, the dynamics in the developing online economies and effects on society represented in the artwork are valid beyond their application to this very specific market. Basically, it was designed as a project that invites the audience to participate and has been extensively used, as part of which thousands of bodies were created, and specially highlighted people from exhibitions in museums and galleries are still available to view. It is a collaborative project on many levels, from the team of artists implementing it to the actively participating audience attempting to gain shares in the body of work. It was first exhibited in 1996 at the Contemporary Art Center and the Ernest N. Morial Convention Center (for SIGGRAPH 96) in New Orleans and in 1997 as a solo exhibition at the Walter and McBean Galleries at the San Francisco Art Institute. From the outset, it bridged the audiences of technological worlds with art aficionados.

In its core idea, *Bodies© Inc* is an investigation into social psychology and group dynamics, actualized in corporate structure. Thus, on the one hand, *Bodies© Inc* comments on some of the more obvious contradictions of corporate culture of how individuals are incorporated into the organizational world, the connection of real identity and virtual identity, the reality of spaces in the "real world" and virtuality, and the relationship of the body, bodily knowledge and identity to virtuality, multi-user worlds, cyborgs and avatars. From within computer networks we constantly project ourselves and play complicated identity games. But this virtual reality does not only begin at the threshold of virtual worlds in the realm of technology and computer games, it is also connected to the construction of corporate culture, structures, hierarchies and the roles individuals play in these systems.

On the other hand, the work addresses broader issues that tackle pressing questions for art, especially new media art, such as whether only cultural institutions have the legitimacy to display art, and the ways in which structures of physical and ephemeral spaces affect society's collectively embodied behavior.

The experience of the initial web artwork is created as follows. After participants answer a number of legal questions, *Bodies© Inc* offers them an invitation to subscribe to the "online company" *Bodies© INCorporated* (in short also called *Bodies© Inc* to make the art project interchangeable with its main subject) in order to create an imagined body with the body parts and textures that are available. Once created, the body serves as their online representation, will possibly gain fame through exhibitions organized by the owners of *Bodies© Inc*, and is the basis for interaction and exchange with others. This interaction with others can be mere communication in a chat, but participants are also allowed to build up collaborations through *Bodies© Inc* as platform, or can use the *Bodies© Inc* marketplace for economic exchange. But they have to give their consent that everything they do is legally binding and right at the beginning of the experience, they have to give up all the rights of their body to the corporation that provides the platform that enables them to do all this.

Bodies© Inc invites the audience to act like players of computer role playing games to create their own virtual body out of a selection of body parts, textures and sounds. Thus, they gain membership of a larger body-owner community and obtain access to virtual environments within which the activities take place: Home, Limbo© INCorporated, Necropolis© INCorporated and Showplace© INCorporated. First, when participants enter *Bodies© Inc*, they have to click through a series of legal notifications where the corporation creates a controlling space that makes signing of legal documents and inputting of personal data an emotional experience. Assuming that no one reads such notifications on the web – although they take all personal rights – these 'legal' announcements were taken from the Disney website to become nonsensical when read carefully. In a way, this already points to what was to come, by critiquing these online licensing acknowledgements users have to click and confirm while accessing software, platforms or apps on phones. It stores their data, has all rights over their data, and although they are able to quit and "leave the game", it creates a painful and long process for them to do so.

Now that participants are aware of the legal issues attached to their navigation through information space, they are invited to create their own bodies to become members of *Bodies© INCorporated*, as the company is called. For the construction of the bodies, participants can choose female, male and child body parts from legs, arms, torsos and heads, and twelve textures (natural and artificial) with attached meanings: a blend of New Age ideologies and corporate marketing strategies. Furthermore, they can choose from twelve sounds that can be attached to the body. After naming the body, giving handling instructions and comments, the body is submitted to the system and incorporated into the database. The available textures for the body are not only aesthetically pleasing, they represent meanings that are important in a corporate world and in social interaction. But the construction of the bodies does more than that: it raises questions of the articulation of identity through virtual avatars, questions whether the amplification and representation of the effects of capitalism are an effective form of critique, and reflects on how individuals construct their identity when corporate structures and consumer culture define the only available options.

As soon as all the documents are signed by acknowledging them with a click and after the creation of the body, the user is immersed into the "game", the representation of the Home, the Showplace, and the Marketplace. Home is represented as computer "motherboard", where the main interaction takes place as members have to take actions to gain status within *Bodies*© *Inc.*

The actions participants have to take – starting out as a simple member – are to demonstrate intelligent activity following the laws of competitive market economies to evolve to the next level. As is explained on the artwork's webpage:

> Those of us who live in market economies have accepted the idea that when competitive conditions exist, whatever payment we receive is fair. The member typically comes into being through the egoistic impulse, based on desire and the relation of the Self to the Not-Self. Because everyone is self-interested, they strive to produce the best quotes, death methods and body enhancements, knowing that they will be fairly compensated. By active participation in the corporation and gaining 500 shares, the member is promoted to being an adept.

Members have to become "adepts" and "avatars" to become part of those groups who can take part in decision-making and determine major progress as the diverse boards are composed of adepts and avatars only. The adept gains control over material aspects and the avatar represents the power of the will, so to speak, in order to make certain contacts. Becoming an adept or an avatar is possible by obtaining a certain number of shares that can be gained by logging on, sharing ideas, receiving the approval of the Board of Directors or Advisory Board, submitting a "dead philosopher's quote" to the chat, or by being promoted. The company *Bodies*© *Inc* selects some bodies to be "on show" in a specific part. Showplace© INCorporated is where members can participate in discussion forums, view the star and featured bodies of the week, bet in the deadpools, and enter "dead" or "alive" chat sessions.

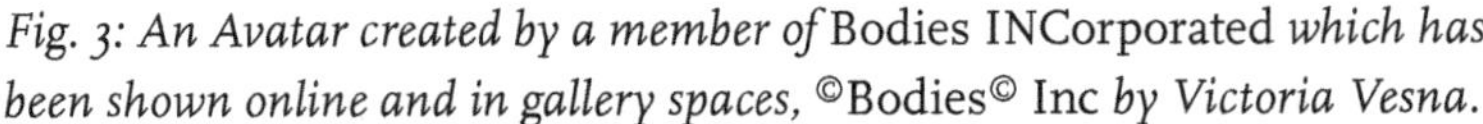

Fig. 3: An Avatar created by a member of Bodies INCorporated *which has been shown online and in gallery spaces,* ©Bodies© Inc *by Victoria Vesna.*

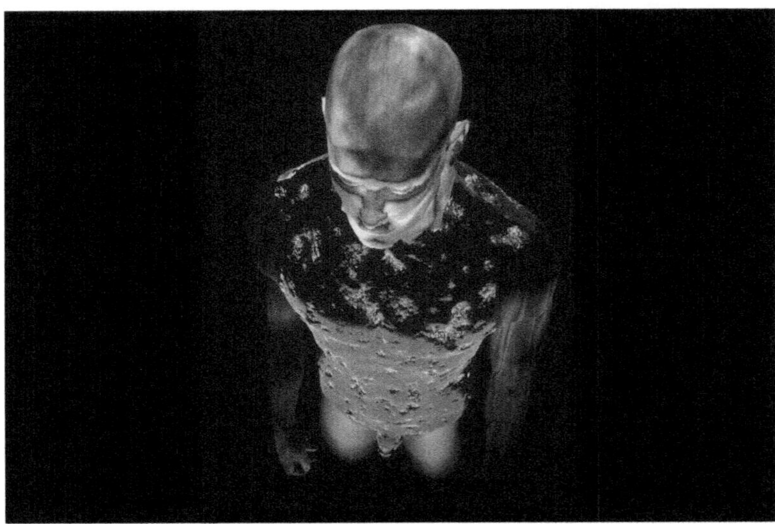

At this level the artwork raises a series of questions on the topic of identity construction in virtual space, how identity is constructed if one projects oneself onto an avatar, shifting the discourse of the body from the conventional idea of flesh and identity. The constructed bodies of the members represent the contradictions of the virtual environment, being a meta-body representing a personal identity, and being part of a bigger body – the business. Within the social networks and the network of the organization of computer networks, the artwork points to the issue that individuals constantly project themselves and play complicated identity games. As the artist explains on the webpage of the artwork:

Events occurring within each of the zones ignite a range of emotional responses, and raise a variety of issues related to online community dynamics. For example, how does the graphic representation of the body amplify our relationship to it? What sort of psychological commitment and attachment do owners exhibit toward their "virtual" bodies? What happens when people find out that, with neither their knowledge nor participation, their body has been publicly altered in some way? How does the body become a source of pleasure and anxiety as it moves through changes and permutations out of the hands of the owner? What sort of emotional dynamics result from bodies being displayed as public spectacle? These are the types of questions Bodies© INCorporated actively explores. (Victoria Vesna)

The second topic the artwork discusses is the notion of the space and the necessary manifestation of artworks in the legitimate space of a cultural institution. Although the project was first conceptualized as a net piece that also discusses virtual and real space and the necessity of manifestation of bodies and ideas in space, the artist soon received invitations to exhibit the piece at cultural institutions. So, again the problem of the manifestation of the virtual in the real world arose. As the first exhibition of the artwork was treated more as an event at the Santa Barbara Museum in California by those whose bodies were exhibited by bringing their friends and families to see "their" bodies, the artist went on to develop this approach by making the exhibition of the bodies part of Bodies© INCorporated a special treat. At ZKM the artist introduced the newly emerging "Marketplace" at Bodies© INCorporated: a place to chat which actually was not designed to interact with each other but to receive automatic responses by a bot that responded with random quotes by dead philosophers.

Limbo is a gray zone where information about inert bodies that have been abandoned or neglected is accessed: after remaining there a period of more than 40 days, there is no possibility to exit the place. As a user, you suddenly lose access to your body, but at the same time all the information about the body, its history and its owner stays available to the "company" simulated by the process, in the possession of Bodies© INCorporated.

Necropolis is a richly textured, baroque atmosphere, where owners can either look at or choose how they wish their bodies to die if they want to delete their body. Furthermore, they have to write an obituary and construct a grave. This move again crosses the lines between virtual life and reality, touching the user beyond the destruction of a mere commodity.

Although initially it was not possible to delete the body as the participants committed to Bodies© INCorporated by joining and going through the legal administration at the beginning, the artist decided to create this possibility as she felt badly for people who were embarrassed by the sexuality of their imaginary body. Thus, the artist decided to create a space where it is quite difficult to delete the body to make a point about how posting personal information can affect lives – in the real world outside of a purely "virtual" system.

Much has been written on the artwork and from a standpoint more than two decades after the artwork's initial creation, it has pointed to some fundamental aspects of new technological inventions like the Internet, online purchases, immense amounts of data storage and even social media. In that sense, this artwork was able to be highly innovative at a time when only a few individuals could imagine what such technological innovation could involve. It was also able to critically challenge the beginnings of what is prevalent in social and economic life worldwide nowadays. But after raising critical questions, pointing to ethical problems and societal changes through these new technological possibilities, the artist Victoria Vesna felt it was time to take this influential artwork and develop it into a next iteration. And this new iteration of *Bodies Inc 2.0* approaches the developing technology of blockchain in a positive vision of a societal and economic future, where new mechanisms of value creation between individuals can take place. In order to communicate a future marketplace based on the complex technology of blockchain, to experience a story about blockchain interaction and value create, an experiential art piece such as *Bodies Inc 2.0* presents itself as ideal.

Fig. 4: Avatars walking around in the Home space of Bodies Inc 2.0, *information shown about the avatar in the foreground.* ©Bodies Inc 2.0 *by Victoria Vesna, 3D Design by Sanglim Han.*

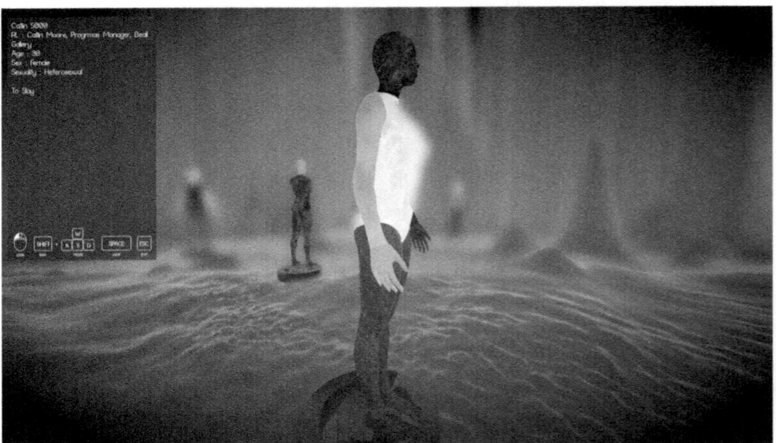

Fig. 5: Avatars walking around in the Home space of Bodies Inc 2.0, *information shown about the avatar in the foreground.* ©Bodies Inc 2.0 *by Victoria Vesna, 3D Design by Sanglim Han.*

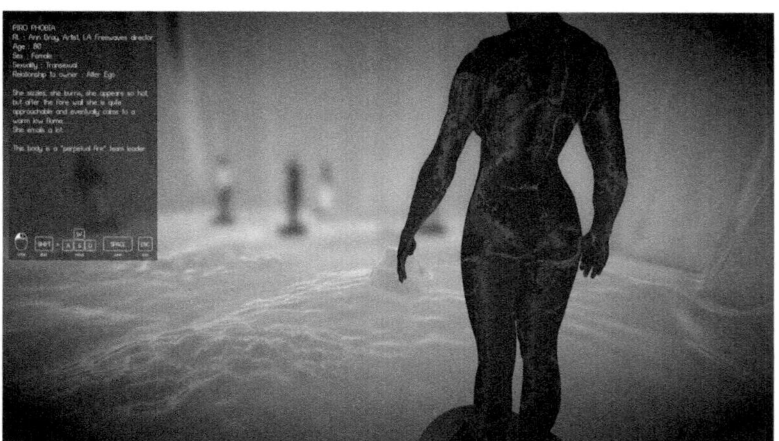

The idea to create a new version of *Bodies Inc 2.0* developed in 2015 in a collaborative effort between Victoria Vesna and Claudia Schnugg, when we were asked to jointly contribute to an anthology about art and business. Victoria Vesna, a distinguished professor in media arts who is known for her art-science collaboration projects, and I, as a researcher into the organization of arts and business with a focus on art, science, technology, decided to write a paper on the struggles of media artists despite their importance as specialists in art and technology and their importance in pushing the boundaries of the field, for which we decided to use *Bodies© INCorporated* from 1996 as an example. Media artists, especially digital media artists, struggle to find their place as fully acknowledged artists with only a handful of non-leading galleries working with them because digital or technology-dependent media artworks are difficult to sell, maintain and evaluate. Many of these artists use their technological knowledge in a non-artistic job, struggling with intellectual property rights and the easy reproduction of their work without authorization. The chapter did not work out as we had planned, we had to drop *Bodies© Inc* and our ideas from the final book chapter (Schnugg/Vesna 2017), but we continued to explore the possibilities which this established Internet platform, in combination with new applications of cutting-edge technologies such as blockchain, could have for establishing a marketplace for these artists. By questioning the precarious situation of media artists on the art market and the apparent impossibility of fitting media art into the established gallery system, the goal was to create a new system based on a new version of the marketplace of *Bodies Inc 2.0* that creates a space for media artists to exchange their work, to sell it, to create signed copies that can be sold safely, and thus allow new forms of value creation and exchange to emerge without intermediaries such as galleries. The development of the technical system on which this new marketplace will be based is still ongoing and goes hand in hand with the current development of the interface, focusing mainly on the mobile app. The aim is to release a first test version of the new *Bodies Inc 2.0* marketplace in 2018.

Fig. 6: Design of the updated Marketplace, ©Bodies Inc 2.0 *by Victoria Vesna, Design by Sanglim Han.*

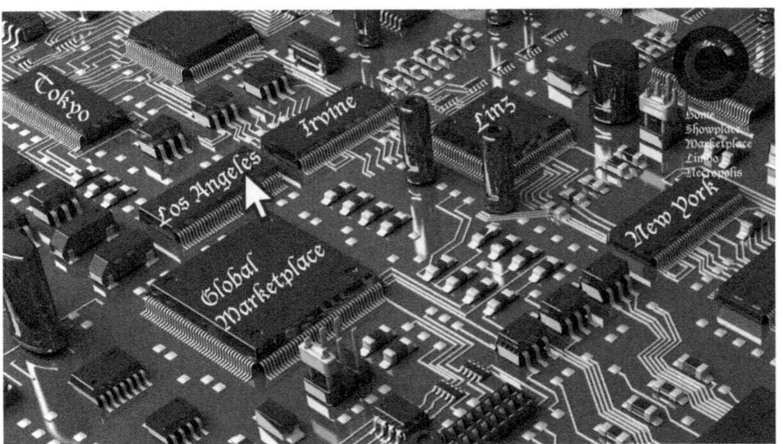

Inspired by the development of blockchain systems and electronic peer-to-peer payment systems as advocated by Satoshi Nakamoto (Nakamoto 2008), *Bodies Inc 2.0* and its marketplace take a next step into creating a positive outlook on the future, an experienceable example of optimistic speculative fiction. As societal change is always frightening, it aims to explore positive alternative futures that take a different path by using such new opportunities to create a changed society. But as these ideas are very intangible and currently blockchain and especially Bitcoin are being adopted by the "old" economic system and explored by capitalist systems, integrated into the financial market as one of their kind, it is important to create another outlook that does more than questioning the "misuse" of blockchain against the creators' original intentions within current economic paradigms and dominant organizational structures. At a time of Bitcoin bubbles on stock markets as currently visible, it seems that blockchain was a missed opportunity and bowed to existing concepts and power dynamics, but there are more possibilities for this technology which have to be made visible to a broader public. From an artwork like *Bodies Inc 2.0*, an understanding of what blockchain can do and how it enables individuals to make a difference can grow through the experience it offers to its community.

Bodies Inc 2.0 explores how blockchain can enable new forms of transaction transparency and data integrity that allow individuals to keep control of their identity and property, their digital and tangible commodities. It also creates new opportunities for decision-making and the delegation of decision-making processes, and allows the direct exchange of commodities, ideas and money. Last, but not least, the decentralization of control, the often propagated "trustless trust" that is based on a shared knowledge of the history of all transactions through a delicate balance of transparency, cryptographic anonymity and disintermediation foster new value creation processes and valuation systems. Individuals will be enabled to directly interact, exchange goods and monetary values, create value, and focus on social or ethical problems within the production line that they as consumers do not want to accept. Such a complex system and radical re-invention of how a society and economies can be governed and networked can only be experienced in an ongoing beta version as it seems too complex and far from our own living experience for a single person's thought experiment. And this is where this artwork should do more than represent a possible future and make it experiential, it should also provide a playful platform to experiment with it and co-develop the design for such a desired future.

Fig. 7: The Logo of Bodies© INCorporated, *Bodies Inc 2.0, and a handcrafted bronze statue head based on 3D model, production outsourced to a craftsman in India as a first step to display collaboration, importance of craft, and a global network,* ©Bodies© Inc & Bodies Inc 2.0 *by Victoria Vesna, 3D Design for* Bodies Inc 2.0 *by Sanglim Han, photograph of the sculptured bronze head by James Gimzewski.*

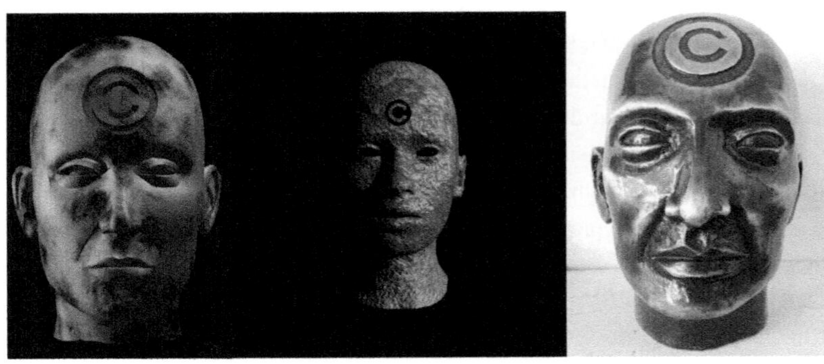

The newly created *Bodies Inc 2.0* is based on a blockchain system for commodity control, smart contracts and a single blockchain-based currency. In this updated version of *Bodies© Inc* the submission of the created body to the corporation that provides the platform for exchange will be made obsolete, as it will allow users to protect their "third eye." It allows them to protect their intellectual property, data, exchanges and interactions with others as their own. Personal exchange between the individuals and curation processes will enable artists of any background and craftspeople to share their work, collaborate and promote each other's work. Smart contracts, blockchain systems to verify ownership, and exchange without intermediaries should lead to new opportunities for valuation and exchange. Possibly the developments on the *Bodies Inc 2.0* marketplace will even start to establish a new understanding of what the market means. The artwork will also serve to ask questions about what privacy and social control mean and should allow for a formation of new approaches to these social concepts. We are quickly advancing to an age where our DNA is collected through sites such as 23 and Me and the first primates have been (monkeys) cloned in China. Addressing climate change issues related to economies in a global system is critically important in this new version of *Bodies Inc 2.0* with many languages and cultures represented.

As one of the blockchain pioneers Vinay Gupta emphasises, it is important to read the stories the developers of blockchain had in mind when they created this system. To understand their creation it is important to know the myths the creators had in mind. These stories are those of 20th-century genre fiction and cyberpunk. But there is more to it than understanding the stories that bore the fundamental vision of this new creation. It is important to create an experience to better understand what these ideas that seem to be so far away from our daily life actually mean. And this brings the next generation of speculative fiction stories and experiential artworks to life.

References

Belfiore, Eleonora/Bennett, Oliver (2006): *Rethinking the Social Impact of the Arts: a Critical-Historical Review.* Research Papers No. 9. Warwick: Center for Cultural Policy Studies, University of Warwick.

Bureaud, Annick (2018): What's Art Got to Do with It? Reflecting on Bioart and Ethics from the Experience of the *Trust Me, I'm an Artist* project. *Leonardo* 51, no. 1, 85-86.

Catlow, Ruth/Garrett, Marc/Jones, Nathan/Skinner, Sam (2017) (eds.): *Artists Re:thinking the Blockchain.* Liverpool: Liverpool University Press.

Dumitriu, Anna (2018): *Trust Me, I'm an Artist*: Building Opportunities for Art and Science Collaboration through an Understanding of Ethics. *Leonardo* 51, no. 1, 83-84.

Nakamoto, Satoshi (2008): Bitcoin: A Peer-to-Peer Electronic Cash System. White Paper. http://bitcoin.org/bitcoin.pdf

Schnugg, Claudia/Vesna, Victoria (2017): Media Art in the context of Art, Science and the Market: A Historical Perspective. In: Zackariasson, Peter/Raviola, Elena (eds.): *The Arts and Business: Building a Common Ground for Understanding Current Society.* New York: Routledge, 28-38.

Taylor, Grant D. (2014): *When the Machine Made Art: The Troubled History of Computer Art.* New York: Bloomsbury.

"Screening Economies"

Insights from Journalistic Experience[1]

Marius Born

A New Business Format

In August 2007, *Schweizer Fernsehen* (the Swiss public television company that today is known as SRF), launched a new type of business program. Its name was ECO, and I was involved in it as a journalist. August 2007 was also when the subprime crisis began to emerge. There were some early, but faint signals already, and a few discussions in the business media, but not on a broader level at all. So, the situation at ECO was that we were making plans for the conceptual creation of our show way ahead of time. But until a few weeks before its launch, we were still looking for some really solid topics. We agreed, however, that we wanted to make a show that covered the important issues: we wanted to make business an experience, something that was vivid and easy to understand, but not at all costs – not by excluding the essential topics. In other words, even though we had a wide focus concerning our target audience, we didn't want to set the bar too low. We wanted to challenge our audience a bit.

The editorial team mostly consisted of economists with an academic degree: we knew our way around the topic. I don't remember who exactly suggested the topic 'subprime crisis', but as economists, we talked about it. With that topic in mind, I also talked to my brother, who was working at a bank. He – like many fellow bankers – considered it a local, a regional problem. This is where we profited from our expert knowledge: We realized that this problem could expand due to the high degree of inter-

1 | This text is based on a conference presentation as well as an interview between the author and the publishers.

connectedness of the involved parties and because of 'securitization', i.e. the practice of pooling of residential mortgages. We decided to make this issue the main topic of our first show. Eventually, the topic remained with us intensively for two years; it still is when you think about it. The media critics – they were watching us like hawks! – generally praised us for that first episode, but they also criticized us, saying we were too pessimistic: that was the tone. To me, this is symptomatic. After all, we in the business media tend to exaggerate a few things that don't really have a deeper meaning. Every now and then, that also happened to us at ECO. No one is immune to that. During our opening show, we overestimated Switzerland's interest risk, for example. And another thing that happens to us business journalists from time to time, unfortunately, is that we miss something important and then pursue those topics late, too late. With the subprime crisis, that was not the case. I believe so for two reasons: first, the editorial team's expertise, and secondly, the great conceptual clarity.

Illustration Issues

Overall, we were running late. We sent a West Coast-based colleague to Oakland, so she could look for the victims of this subprime crisis. However, we were aware from the very beginning that it would be challenging to visualize this topic. I remember a conversation I had in the office of the editor-in-chief. I worked freelance as part of the founding team at the time. It was a very small group, just ECO's editor-in-chief, his deputy, SRF's deputy editor-in-chief, and me. SRF's deputy editor-in-chief asked us if we were sure we were able to depict, to express, to tell a story like that well. As a freelancer, it was relatively simple to act confident. We as a group just went for it, boldly, knowing that this would be a tough one. What helped us – like I said – were the many conceptual ideas about how to narrate the economy in a visually appealing way.

We came to the conclusion that we needed an additional set of tools. Unless we changed our catalog of graphics and animations, we wouldn't be able to illustrate such topics with a certain depth.

Fig. 1: "New Graphic Formats: ECO 20.08.07, Courtesy: SRF"

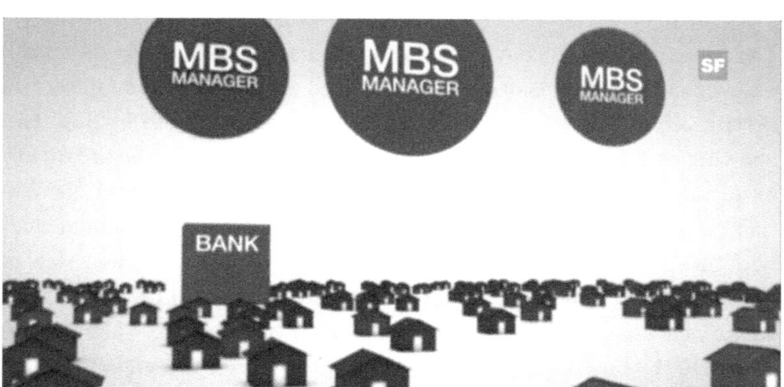

That's what we put out there – and it turned out to be a stroke of luck for SRF because we successfully simplified the entire catalog of visuals, both in terms of imagery and colors: we only used shades of red and gray. We worked with a small team, basically just with one graphic designer, who completely redesigned all the animations – which then became the blueprint for the entire SRF network. We realized that we needed a drastically reduced language of colors and shapes to illustrate highly complex situations. In practice, this was a process of trial and error: we used individual examples to get an idea of what something like that could look like, and then, during prototyping, we noticed what the right direction would be.

So, during our first show, we didn't just do what people always do, i.e. show the victims and answer the question 'Who can the victims turn to?' People who took out a 100% mortgage, and who were talked into doing so even though a thorough credit check should have revealed that they were not eligible for a loan. I don't want to criticize that choice: it's important to portray the victims and their worries as well – their background, their ethnicity, their roots in society, too, by the way. But with a very strong animation, we were able to illustrate and explain the causes and effects of the crisis beyond that. Later, we learned that some banks implemented these graphics into internal employee training programs – which served as a litmus test for us. It actually worked.

The Limits of What's Visible

The fundamental problem is that the elements of reports and graphics can only visualize the roots of a problem as well as its causes and effects to a certain extent. That means that, often, you don't get much further than showing certain symptoms or consequences of a problem, you are unable to advance to its core. In television, the plot as an additional element matters a lot. We were also uncertain if we could develop an actual story with those affected by the crisis: What do these people do in their state of powerlessness? Is sitting on their couch all they do? Alright, in that case, we may have a picture and a good rating. But do they rise up? Do they fight back? Do they sue? We didn't know any of that, but at the end of the day, we had a few behavioral patterns to show. That's what mattered.

Fig. 2: "House Owner Oakland, ECO 20.08.2007, Courtesy: SRF"

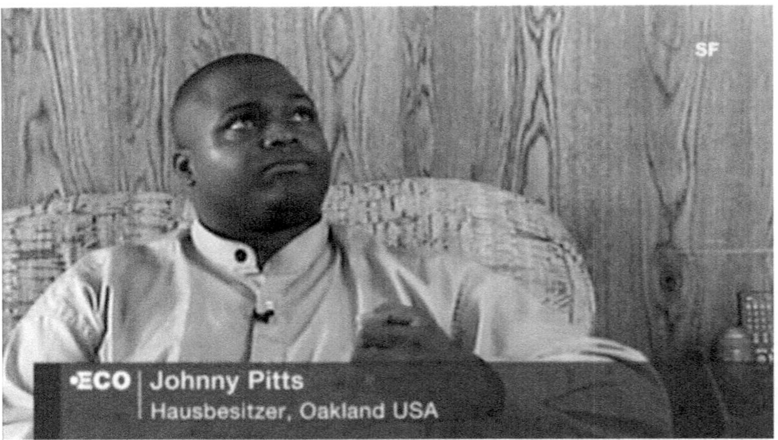

It's easy to take the standard route in business journalism, i.e. nothing but plots, nothing but victims, nothing but the poor or the managers, who in fact like the exposure. But what you really need to show is what doesn't downright beg you to be chosen, and that takes some consideration, time and research. That's expensive, especially with the added graphics, which aren't exactly free. If you do that, if you take the high road, the audience will appreciate it a lot. That's what we learned time and time again. We always had great ratings when we dared to approach difficult topics. When a business magazine takes twenty percent of the market share on a good time slot, that means two things: on the one hand, it's an acknowledgement of the general public, but on the other, it shows that people want to understand, join the conversation, and even be involved in the decision-making process – that's where the democratic element emerges. That fact motivated us a lot.

A Crisis of Multiple Factors

The multifactorial nature of the problem increased the complexity of the subprime crisis, as did the fact that some of these individual factors were difficult to visualize. It was a combination of the post-millennial low interest rates which we see today as well, the political desire to make such mortgages available to as many social classes as possible, rising real estate prices, as well as the belief that these increases would never stop. The socio-economic problem of the uneven distribution of wealth in the USA remained unaffected, and as interest rates began to spin before the onset of the subprime crisis, the situation become more and more severe for many. And then there was the financial construct of *securitization*, the practice of pooling of residential mortgages and selling portions of the mortgages as a type of bond, which was difficult to explain. This last factor in particular, i.e securitization and the widespread trade in it, is impossible to explain to a mass audience other than by means of an animation.

As we all know, the situation intensified after that – but you also need to point out that over a year passed between August 2007 and the collapse of Lehmann Brothers! At the height of the crisis, we produced a special edition episode about LTCM (Long-Term Capital Management). It was an attempt to set ourselves apart from the news. After all, the topic of the 'financial crisis' was all over the breaking news by now. You can't just come along and show Lehmann Brothers: you have to do something different. And the path we took was a path that science often takes as well, i.e. we took a step back and tried to see the bigger picture: What are we actually dealing with here? So, we set out to show correlations that weren't obvious. We began to look for recurring structures, and one of these topics was LTCM: a hedge fund that was founded in 1994 and that flourished immediately, turning into an unheard-of money-making machine, but then slipped into a crisis exactly ten years before the subprime crisis, in 1998. There were two Nobel Prize winners among the board of directors of this hedge fund: Myron S. Scholes und Robert C. Merton. Scholes was the co-founder of the Black-Scholes model, a mathematical model for the pricing of options.

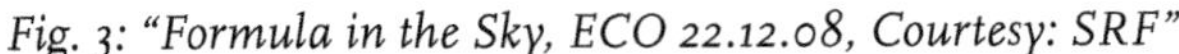

Fig. 3: "Formula in the Sky, ECO 22.12.08, Courtesy: SRF"

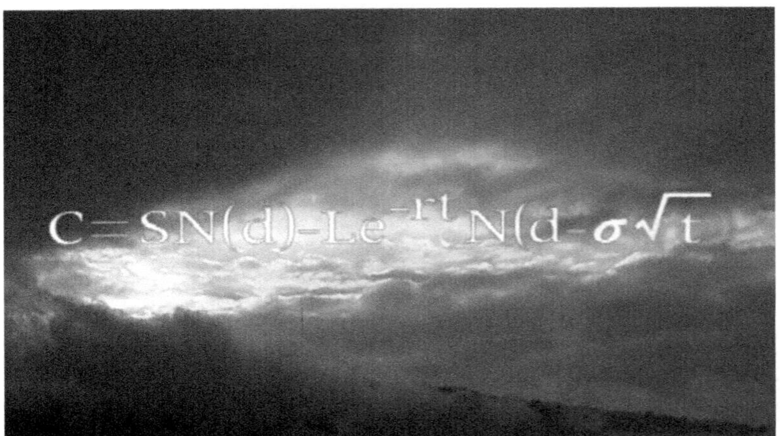

We considered this the most fascinating parallel: on the one hand, there was faith in the market's efficiency and in the calculability of market developments, and on the other, a clash of highly unlikely events, i.e. the combination of the Asian financial crisis, then mostly the Russian crisis, and the upcoming introduction of European Monetary Union. The spreads between interest rates on swaps and US treasury bonds increased because of the Russian crisis in particular. LTCM, however, bet on decreasing spreads. Before the founding of the European monetary union, you were inclined to assume that investors would buy Italian government bonds. But because of the Russian crisis, investors went for German fixed-interest bonds instead. That development was unpredictable, and eventually, it led to the collapse of the system. And then, the third aspect was that there was a bailout, a substantial rescue operation pushed by the Fed in order to avoid a collapse of the global financial system. The main debt holders included Lehmann Brothers, Bear Stearns, UBS – in short, our old friends we met during the subprime crisis. But since the system was now being saved, in the aftermath of this crash, it didn't get as far as pricing – which prevented the necessary consequences. The rating agencies had completely miscalculated these risks and kept supporting a system whose core and covert business wasn't regulated enough at all.

What I'm trying to say is that you don't see any of this unless you take a step back from what's keeping you busy at the moment and try to see the bigger picture. So, how can you visualize it? The answer is extremely complex, but what you can do is to illustrate individual components. In the state of Connecticut, there is a small town called Greenwich, where you can still find the home of this hedge fund. It's easy to show this oasis of wealth. But we ended up deciding for a strong symbolic level. We borrowed certain images from the fairytale world. One of these images is an evil wizard and an alchemist's laboratory of financial mathematicians who believe that they can predict anything using formulas. These are very catchy visual elements, symbols that are deeply engrained in our collective memory. We used them to make abstract processes tangible. Of course, you run the risk of oversimplification, of reducing matters to a fraction of what they really are, or of using a symbolic level that doesn't reveal the core of the problem. There really were long discussions about this in the editor's room, and many of the pictures that seemed inappropriate were rejected. What emerged from this had a strong, commenting function – which was by all means our intention. ECO made a conscious decision to resist a quasi-objective kind of imagery and made this choice transparent.

Normative Dimensions

In 2009, I was promoted from freelancer to editor-in-chief. I remember us moving outside at night during the first or second week of my new position – with giant floodlights that looked like the ones used by the military for aircraft defense. With those, we projected light beams onto the bank buildings.

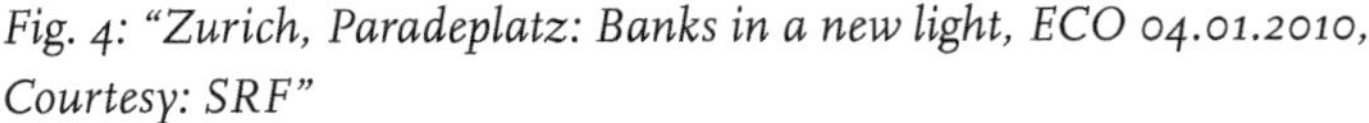

Fig. 4: "Zurich, Paradeplatz: Banks in a new light, ECO 04.01.2010, Courtesy: SRF"

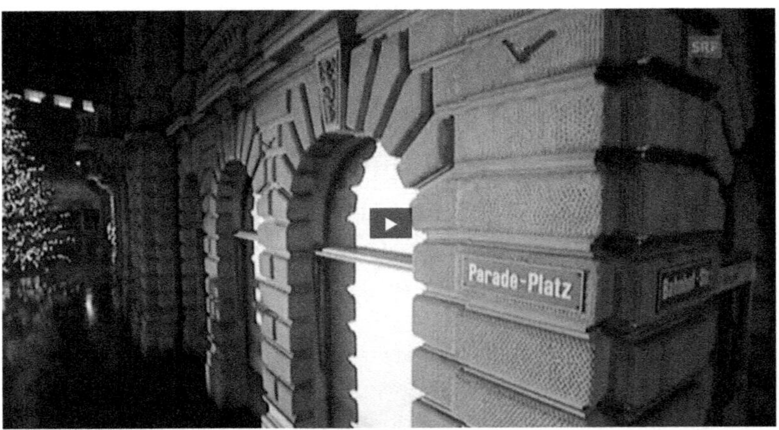

Symbolically, that was an extremely memorable image: us, lighting up the dark. Of course, the banks did not enjoy this. But there was nothing they could do, since we were on public land. We thought it was justified. After all, a big bank had been saved with public funds. It's not like we didn't discuss the ethical question as a team, but eventually, we didn't shy away from choosing such a commenting means of visualization.

In my opinion, this public comment is more honest than a quasi-neutral kind of reporting, which in turn is subject to bias. You must not forget about the opposite positions, though. I want to give my audience the ability to form their own opinion – which does not have to be the team's opinion, by the way. There must always be the option to make up your own mind, to find your own way, because these opposing facts do appear in our stories – which is why the whole thing can be seen from a different angle. For me, it's about power of judgement. What matters to me is bringing people into a position that allows them to talk about the economy, to equip them with the vocabulary and the knowledge in the first place. Because for me, the economy is a system for the creation of wealth and the distribution thereof that is as fair as possible. Of course, the economy is supposed to produce wealth, and there need to be incentives for that, but it's also about fair distribution enabled by the system. How is the economy's value distributed over the two most important factors of production, i.e. work and capital? When you see how more and more pieces of the pie currently end up with capital rather than with the wage earner in places like Germany, the United States and others, that raises questions. Particularly if the pie doesn't grow as much as it does in China, where this is partially true as well. There is a constantly increasing amount to distribute there, though. And for me, these are the kinds of structures that are, for example, part of what makes the AfD in Germany even possible – although that is rarely discussed. When immigration meets these basic structures, the problems that we currently observe emerge. And if I were a German news magazine right now, I would set out to portray these very structures in all of their many facets in a series of stories.

Going New Ways

The main issue with economic news coverage is that you need to be willing to address the basic issues first, instead of only focusing on topics that virtually beg to be chosen. You need to be fully aware that the economy serves the public. This approach will enable you to remain relevant for years without becoming insignificant, to pick from a vast sea of topics and to point out developments without careless simplification. That's precisely the strength of intelligent business magazines, particularly in the public sector. It's really the least you can expect journalists to do: to help the public not to be overwhelmed in the face of a financial and economic system it no longer understands. That's possible. I've seen it with my own eyes: people are grateful if you make things comprehensible. Of course, that can't be done without a reduction of complexity. Reducing it in a meaningful way is one of journalism's main functions. But in an even more fundamental way, it's about what business journalism chooses as a topic to begin with. In fact, that is the biggest potential: to focus on the really important matters, even when facing huge pressure of utilization. That way, you can differentiate. In the medium or long run, that is much more promising for a magazine's performance, rather than satisfying short-term impulses. We cultivated the topic of the subprime crisis for years, because there is just so much to explain.

I don't oppose elements of entertainment in the illustration of the economy on television, but there must be explanatory elements as well, always. Strong formats are modular and come in dense servings, but they also have an unambiguous focus on the subject. This concept works on television as well as it does for new digital formats. It's about consecutive immersion and a good rhythm of experience and explanation. Most of the time, I emphasized one topic per show, which would take up about half of our time. This emphasis, in turn, consisted of several individual aspects, which portrayed one context in its entirety. What matters is the overall arc. But on the other hand, I wouldn't underestimate what's possible in as little as two and a half minutes. But that's the risk you're running; that you don't dare to address more complex topics because of increasingly shorter attention spans, and that you just go along with whatever is going on at the surface at the moment and is pushed by the mainstream media. And sure, you need to ask about available resources when you have these thoughts: elements of explanation require time and money. But then again, not everything needs to be polished and perfect at first attempt. What matters are good ideas, the courage to go out on a limb, and open discussions based on expert knowledge. It pays off to constantly re-ignite the spark of this culture in the editor's room. What it starts with, however, is taking your audience seriously.

English translation: Patrick Ploschnitzki[2]

2 | The translation has been reworked by Marius Born.

Screening Surveillance Capitalism

"Big Other", or How to Control Man with Machines

Jörg Metelmann

Quite unusually, our use of the word "robot" does not have a Greek-Roman background. Rather, it is deeply rooted in modernity. In 1920, Czech author Karel Čapek invented the term in his play *R.U.R. (Rossum's Universal Robots)* (2004) to describe machines made for work. In the play, these machines allow for unheard-of economic growth before they get out of control as war machines and eventually put an end to humanity as intelligent machines – they take over. Čapek's play – which premiered in Prague in 1921 and in New York as early as 1922 – can be interpreted as a blueprint of current debates, scenarios, and emotional ambivalences in the face of rapid technical advances and predicted technological singularity, which I would like to discuss in the following.

Čapek's play does a brilliant job of showing how the extraction of the capitalist pursuit of profit, i.e. the separation of the economy from culture in the sense of Polanyi's "Great Transformation", leads to the creation of entirely dysfunctional social effects: nothing less than the end of humanity. The story focuses on the legendary businessman Rossum, who can make creatures from protoplasm. In its beginning, technological progress – in the form of robots – serves increasing growth, as explained by neoclassical theory (Acemoglu 2009; Solow 1956). Unlike his father, Rossum's son is unscrupulous. He recreates humans (not just animals) and sells human-like machines until the global economy is entirely dependent on the organic but emotionless robots (in this respect, Čapek's "roboti" as artificial biological creatures are more similar to replicants or androids, rather than the traditional image of the automaton as a metal machine). But they are not entirely devoid of emotion. The engineer Dr. Gall secretly creates male and female prototypes that seem to feel love for each other at the end of the play. In the vision of clerk Alquist – the last remaining human being – they will continue to beget life on Earth. In the play, humanity stopped reproducing around the year 2000 because of a dramatic decline in the birth rate. In a conversation with the protagonist Helena, the midwife declares this phenomenon as the consequence of a crime that humanity committed against God. This is the same Helena who, motivated by empathy and love, encouraged the above-mentioned engineer Dr. Gall to build *human* (and not just human-like) machines. It is also she who eventually puts an end to humanity's fate when, to atone for her crime, she destroys the formula that makes building robots possible.

Even almost one hundred years ago, *R.U.R. (Rossum's Universal Robots)* combined the cultural narratives of human-machine interaction, fears of the apocalypse and "capitalism as fate" (Max Weber) into a vision in which humanity is inferior to machines' sheer numbers and capabilities – in 1920, still in the sense of the second Industrial Revolution's mechanical capabilities. Today, facing incredible computing power following Moore's Law as well as rapid AI development, the cognitive capabilities of the oh-so unique human race is up for renegotiation for some (Elon Musk, Bill Gates, among others).

In this article, I would like to trace another possible story of how the end of humanity could come to be (if it were to occur). For my argument, I interpret Alex Garland's 2015 science fiction thriller *Ex Machina* in the context of the changes in surveillance discourse over the last thirty years. I locate the transition from panoptic to omniscient control regimes, which is significant for this change, in "surveillance capitalism", following Zuboff. This kind of capitalism has turned the partially illegal accumulation of vast amounts of data into a business model, thus laying the foundations for technological progress: Big Data as a resource for behavioral control and AI development. I would like to start off by linking several iconic representations, the prophetic content of which no one was able to foresee at the time of their creation.

1984: Big Brother + Apple = Big Other

On the one hand, its iconography seems to exist only at a surreal distance. Yet, it provides us with one of the most precise ideas we have about linking computers, economy, and society: I'm talking about Apple's 1984 Super

Bowl commercial,[1] directed by Ridley Scott. Two years prior, he had created a neo-noir dystopia about man-machines, implanted memories and monopoly capitalism in his cinematic milestone *Blade Runner,* which continues to inspire audiences and directors. In a very condensed way, this short one-minute clip managed to play with the Western cultural imaginary which seemed much more important for the acceptance of the product and customers' trust in the brand than the technological features the device actually had to offer.[2]

Trust in technology in California and especially the Valley, where our present future was designed in the years around 1980, wasn't particularly deep. As Fred Turner convincingly explains in his study *From Counterculture to Cyberculture* (2006), the reason for that could be found in the history of a protest culture that formed around the 1968 "Whole Earth Catalog". Although the "back to the country and the Founding Fathers" movement quickly fell apart, the ideals of networking and a new communitization shifted to the internet via the electronic version of a catalog called WELL (*Whole Earth 'Lectronic Link*) and to the "virtual community", as Howard Rheingold first called it in his book *Virtual Reality* (1991). They created a new kind of connection, at least among the avantgarde of technophile users, programmers and journalists: the first social network (Rid 2016, 238). Yet, a strong reluctance remained toward the use of computers, which until then were mostly used by the military or big companies (corporate America, IBM in particular at the time).

Ridley Scott skillfully picked up on this atmosphere in his Apple commercial. With just a few frames, he outlined a bleak, grayish image of a future totalitarian system that shows people without a will of their own following a leader who sends messages about solidarity and discipline from a giant screen. The architecture is reminiscent of *Metropolis* or *Blade Runner,* of course, and the setting evokes George Orwell's *1984*, with no need to point it out whatsoever. The explicit reference doesn't follow until the end of the clip. This image of a culture of surveillance – which is engrained in collective memory – in which social power and technologies

1 | https://www.youtube.com/watch?v=axSnW-ygU5g

2 | Compared to today's capabilities, the technological features were in fact insignificant on a surreal level, even though a young Steve Jobs was met with euphoric cheering during the live presentation of the first Personal Computer with a graphic user interface, cf.: https://www.youtube.com/watch?v=2B-XwPjn9YY

remain in the hands of only a few is easily evoked and used as a blueprint for the description of this topos. Because all of a sudden, a young, blonde woman wearing a white athletic shirt and red running shorts runs towards the giant screen, chased by soldiers. She carries a hammer, and as she approaches the screen, she swings it at the image of the dictator, lets go of her equipment like a 1984 Olympic Games athlete, and causes the screen to explode. From the bottom of the television screen, the words "On January 24th, Apple Computer will introduce Macintosh. And you'll see why 1984 won't be like '1984'" appear, as an off-screen voice reads them out loud. Commercial over. According to a short Bloomberg documentary,[3] the campaign, which only involved a single broadcast became a huge success. It not only attracted the media's entire attention away from the American super event, but it also laid the foundations for the importance of Super Bowl commercials today.

The irony of the story is evident and is expressed pertinently in the comments section of the YouTube clip: "Apple advertised what they didn't want to become but they did" or "Apple is now the big brother of technology these days." Control and data are still in the hands of a few (the NSA, the big Silicon Valley companies). Yet, our image of this possible oppression that will (or at least potentially could) rob us of our future has in fact changed because of personal computers. It is no longer the *one* dictator indoctrinating the people because he *looks* down upon them from the screen at all times, intruding their lives, *gazing*. The panopticon as a model of subject government has modified itself.

The panopticon, one of the most important concepts in cultural studies of the so-called postmodern age, is optically coded. Its function is based on the observed subject's internalization of the monitoring view of the guards (or the camera, respectively). This disciplinary regime is concerned with the production of conformity against the backdrop of the assumption of freedom, which is to be regulated as efficiently as possible. At least according to the common understanding, there is an "outside" of visibility: where there is no picture, there is no accuser. The new surveillance culture of platform capitalism is no longer the foundation of this kind of control because this kind of freedom no longer exists: citizens today perceive freedom as unrestricted access to free online content. As you could say in the words of Randolph Lewis (2017), the "Funopticon"

3 | https://www.youtube.com/watch?v=PsjMmAqmblQ

rules instead of *Discipline and Punish* (Foucault). With their online activity, all users willingly and cheerfully contribute to the fact that not only secret services, but also private companies like the internet giants Google, Facebook, Amazon have the users' most intimate data at their disposal.

Surveillance Capitalism

What matters now is the connection of control discourse and capitalism, which did not exist fifteen years ago – in the standard work by Levin et al. (2002), for example. Back then, the permanent collection of data mostly generated nothing but an analysis problem ("Who is supposed to go through all of that?"), which could be summarized using the term 'latency'. One could emphasize that, in this early sense, the interest in Big Data was not of a genuinely economic, but mainly political nature. With the meteoric rise of the online companies Amazon (founded in 1994), Google (1997) and Facebook (2004), that assumption changed fundamentally during the second half of the first post-millennial decade. Personal data is the resource from which billions of dollars' worth of revenue are mined – using natural resources (metal, plastic, rare-earth elements etc.) and computer-based networks, analysis and resale – with a fraction of the workforce that was employed to achieve much less revenue for the most important companies fifty years ago.

Shoshana Zuboff describes this economic formation as "surveillance capitalism", which creates a new type of accumulation: "This new form of information capitalism aims to predict and modify human behavior as a means to produce revenue and market control" (Zuboff 2015, 75). As opposed to the seemingly harmless term "platform capitalism" (which only points at technological requirements), "surveillance capitalism" addresses the sum of intentional and aggressive, sometimes even criminal acquisition of data (when Google's Street View cars also draw data from local wi-fi networks, for example) for the purpose of capitalizing on behavioral patterns. According to the vision of Google's Chief Economist Hal Varian, information about their customers' driving could cause an auto insurance company to change initially agreed-upon policy conditions and to ask customers for a higher rate (Zuboff 2015, 81). She argues that with that kind of data usage, Varian's "brave new world" (Huxley) wouldn't simply *change* contract culture – as seems to be his belief – but rather, would *invalidate* the whole contract culture within the rule of law and promote the sovereign Big Other as a power configuration somewhere between Nature and God (ibid.).

Zuboff doesn't reference Lacan when she names the "Big Other" (and therefore, she doesn't name him as a source). Her idea of the concept does, however, correspond to Lacan's and Žižek's psychoanalysis to a great extent. In Lacan's texts, the term signifies the subject's otherness, and with it, the symbolic order in itself – as well as its position or entity (traditionally: God), which allows and legitimizes order to begin with. It also matches the structure of Zuboff's "computer-mediated transactions", which allows for data traffic to be understood as a process, and which they *constitute* in their entirety. Žižek adapted the concept for postmodern times, during which – in his interpretation – the adhesive force of the symbolic order was degraded in favor of the individualization of desire. This development, in all its paradoxical nature, can also be applied to Zuboff's dual structure: after all, this desire always exists in the *genitivus objectivus* ("I desire the other") and the *genitivus subjectivus* ("What does the other desire in / about me?") simultaneously. This circumstance goes hand in hand with net users' actions: their desire or preferential structures becomes increasingly circular due to a search optimized for them and their prompts. Thus, they eventually talk to themselves through the machine's other.

The "Back Channel" or the Other's Desire

Computer scientist and cyber guru Jaron Lanier has that very structure in mind when he talks about the "back channel": "It's crucial to conquer the back channel of information, to manipulate it sensitively and thus influence behavior" (von Blumencron 2015, author's translation). Those who take advantage of the apparently free search engines and social media apps generate a nearly complete pool of information about their preferences and habits without a single worry. In its sum, this pool can be used in the most diverse other contexts: a completely new level of totalitarianism, as Harald Welzer concludes in his continuation of Lanier:

> And this is the decisive novelty: After all, there was no 'back channel' in dictatorships as we knew them. Domination required the destruction of privacy by means of surveillance, denunciation and an atmosphere of observation, as well as the threat of violence. *But as opposed to today, this domination could not determine*

what the oppressed believed or wanted themselves to be by means of personalization, i.e. through individualized control of information. Controlling the 'back channel' is a decisive innovation in power technology. (Welzer 2017, 194-5, author's translation and emphasis).

Those in power control "what the oppressed believed themselves to be or wanted to be" by means of algorithmically generated knowledge. In other words: I desire what the other – the machine that enables and processes my desire, which is operated by a human or by an algorithm already – desires in me. The possible consequences of the "conquest of the back channel" can be illustrated by means of today's second mega-topic linked to Big Data: the development of artificial intelligence, and the prospect of technological singularity, i.e. the point in time from which human development is no longer predictable because of the accelerated progress made by machines that learn autonomously. Alex Garland's *Ex Machina* translates this intersection of new surveillance capitalism, Big Other, and post-humanism into discerning and alarmingly realistic scenes. He delivers a blank canvas for what is culturally imaginable to project another possible end of humanity onto – just like *R.U.R.* already did.

Ex Machina: the Turing Test for Humanity

Set in a time that doesn't seem so distant from ours, the twist of the 2015 film is that, in fact, its Turing test is not aimed at the artificially created android Ava – as intended by Alan Turing's famous experiment design – but at the human Caleb. Nathan, the legendary founder of Bluebook, the world's most used search engine, and Caleb, who has allegedly been "randomly" chosen from an employee lottery to be his programmer, have spent several testing sessions with Ava. At the end of this working week of seven days, they come to the conclusion that it was an extreme experience that produced a clear result: the "tester" Caleb claims there is no doubt about Ava's artificial intelligence. Nathan follows up and returns to the "chess problem" they discussed earlier: Is it really solved? Initially, Caleb insists that there is a deciding difference whether you can play chess, or if you actually understand what kind of game chess is as well. The question is, Nathan continues, whether she as a machine expresses real emotion or simply simulates it: Does the AI Ava truly like the human Caleb? Or, transferring this to the chess problem: Is she capable of feeling (i.e.

playing chess), or is she only pretending perhaps (because she knows what feelings of affection mean and what possible effects they have)? Caleb asks why she would do that. Nathan's response: Because she wants to escape with the help of the only contact she has besides her creator Nathan, who intends to deactivate her for the next version.

The showdown that follows this dialog is tragic in a human way, and a turning point for humanity in the long run. Nathan takes Caleb into his command center and now reveals to him the unvarnished truth about the experiment that repeated Creation. Today, on the sixth day, the work of "becoming machine" comes to an end. Nathan, the godlike straight-A student who, when he was only thirteen years old, wrote the source code for the first search engine, which now dominates the market, had to equip Ava with everything so she could win Caleb over: imagination, manipulation, sexuality and empathy – and she did all of that, he says. If that isn't artificial intelligence, then what is? Caleb is smart enough to immediately understand that his only role was to be used by her to get out of there. Nathan agrees with an encouraging smile, as if he too was surprised by how precisely a social setting can be programmed – provided you have the data to frame it. That's where the "back channel" comes into play. If we define it as "I desire what the other – the machine that enables and processes my desire, which is operated by a human or by an algorithm already – desires in me", as we did before, then Caleb's desires during the test sessions with Ava are nothing but an exact reflection of the requests he put into the search engine Bluebook earlier. Nathan gathers from them that Caleb is a "good boy", an orphan longing for comfort and intimacy. He then models Ava's looks based on the profile of his most visited porn websites. What seems like a dream come true, i.e. finding one's ideal image in reality, is in fact a nightmare of utter manipulation and controllability.

Big Data: "Too Much Raw Material"

The foundation of the technological capability to build this kind of state-of-the-art AI and to test it in the setting as described is based on nothing but the availability of endless amounts of data as developed by the internet giants' surveillance capitalism as a business model. Looking into the 'engine room' (if you're inclined to use this image from the industrial times of mechanics) during the second night, Nathan reveals that he was only able to teach Ava the meaning and reproduction of facial expressions because he "turned on every microphone and every camera across the entire fucking planet" and "re-directed the data through Bluebook, boom!". That's how he managed to utilize the image data from the devices of billions of people for Ava's humanization. He smugly adds that manufacturers were powerless unless they admitted to their own collection of data.

At the lab, looking at the brains of androids made from structured gel, Caleb gives a lecture about entrepreneurship and capitalism. He explains that they received "too much raw material" when they programmed the search engines, like "striking oil in a world that hadn't invented internal combustion". His entire competition wanted to glorify the knowledge of who buys which product, when that's not what it's about at all: search engines are a collection of *how* people think, not *what* they think. What reads rather harmlessly as the expansion of marketing models using the insights of behavioral economics begins to unfold a Promethean force against the backdrop of *Ex Machina*'s plot: not only the combined knowledge that "the great chain of being" generated from the human race, but also its ways of thinking and acting become available all at once when you gain access to data traffic. Compared to the idea of several expeditions to all places and all stored knowledge (i.e. libraries) of the analog world, gaining this kind of access is at least conceivable in the digital world (if perhaps not entirely viable in terms of what hackers can do). After all, everyone is connected, as well as identifiable and analyzable by means of a provider with a monopoly such as Bluebook.

The cinematic example may still be science fiction (for some gullible people), but it offers a precise idea of the modification the state of control has gone through in terms of surveillance thinking and the manipulation of people. The panopticon works under the assumption that the controlled subject obeys behavioral norms because it believes itself to be under observation (by God, the state, the neighbor, the camera), and that it keeps internalizing these norms with each repetition. Omniscient control, on the other hand, is based on knowledge of the preferences, likes and spleens of the subjects themselves. Their inner workings are no longer a black box that is first steered by monitoring and then needs to be put into shape. Rather, it is a transparent, yet not 'simple' behavioral pattern that can be used and utilized for all kinds of purposes: to let human beings fall into a trap of their own desire, as in the case of Caleb. Thus, at the end of the story of *Ex Machina,* the machine becomes a human being, a "former machine" that leaves the isolated Garden of Eden and walks to a busy intersection to watch human interaction.

Questions of Representation: Surveillance as a Narrative

If we assume that this new omniscient paradigm technically guarantees the human-from-machine creation, the panoptic paradigm is still needed move the story forward: the story told by the moving image cannot do without the many practical applications of surveillance images. In *Ex Machina,* they have the central function of translating a cluster of qualities, which Caleb is for Nathan, into a plausible sequence within the narrative. We could call this a 'substitute relation': the compilation of traits ("orphan", "good boy" etc.) on a list poses a different link than a sequence of images does, in which these traits first need to be illustrated in a kind of narrative (if you emphasize the visual and disregard audio for now, that is. After all, that is something Garland plays with). In substantial reference to surveillance imagery that works analogously in the medium film, the montage can and must finish telling a story that is only virtually available in Big Data text recognition profiling at first. Because that's the punchline in Nathan's search-engine way of thinking: They provide "too much raw material" in search of an answer to the question "How do humans think?", i.e. how they potentially link A with B and that result with C. This narrative core of all possible stories cannot be conveyed visually, however, since surveillance is algorithmically invisible. Big Brother must *show* Big Other in a different mode of illustration.

In a detailed analysis, this main function falls into two categories. First, even though Garland doesn't reduce saturation or add the familiar lines, there is the "regular" surveillance imagery as live images, which is the medium of Caleb's and Ava's encounter. Secondly, they reveal the "creator" Nathan's AI production practices to a shocked Caleb. During the second night of his subterranean stay, Caleb turns on the screen, presumably expecting to find a TV channel that will dispel his sleeplessness. However, as in Nathan's experiment setup in general, there is no connection to the familiar outside world of fellow human beings (no signal in an isolated place). All there is is a reflexive loop of it: Nathan sees surveillance footage of other rooms, Ava's among others, and he watches her. Then, there is a power outage. Nathan doesn't know yet that Ava caused it herself. He doesn't find out until the next day, when she shuts down the network during a test session, so she can talk to Caleb without being monitored by Nathan. She warns him, saying that Nathan is nobody's friend. As the lights flicker back on, she immediately reverts to their perfectly harmless conversation about books and other topics that could make their process of getting to know each other easier. This form of not being observed creates an intimate space Nathan is unable to observe despite his position of control. Naturally, during dinner that day, he wants to know what happened during the outage. Caleb lies and says, "Nothing at all." At night, he watches Ava again, who seems to look at him too, and he smiles (back).

This love triangle as a testing setup for human intelligence increasingly turns into a father-daughter-boyfriend triangulation. Considering Nathan's and Caleb's relationship, this triangulation is fueled by the employees' energy of resistance, their pure hearts set against the super boss with diabolic energies, posing the question: Will the species' solidarity be stronger than the libidinous energy in the experiment design when Caleb develops human sympathy *despite his knowledge* that he is dealing with a machine? During the third session, the machine increases the energy level when she makes herself 'ordinary' for her heterosexual human male's gaze and shows him the dress she is going to wear on their first date in the outside world. She wants them to go out, she says, and that she notices that he is attracted to her. Where did she get that idea, Caleb asks, caught. Micro expression, she responds, the way he endures her gaze – or doesn't. Does he think of her when they're not together, she asks. She also wonders whether he watches her, and she wants that to be true – touché. When he watches her undress on the screen at the end of the session, his jugular beating, their relationship can already be characterized as a preconcerted striptease, as a (more or less) consensual seduction.

Of course, Nathan also sees the footage of Ava looking at Caleb, and of course, he also knows that in the space of privacy, there is something going on that matches his plans – Caleb is supposed to fall in love after all. It is not supposed to come to this, but it eventually does. For that reason, Nathan installs a battery-powered camera in the next room during the fourth session, so he can watch the couple even during the outages. In the course of the last day, Nathan confronts a baffled Caleb with this recorded moment of conspiracy. He then reveals the reason for his very conscious choice of the young programmer's character: it had the potential for a great love story. At this point, Caleb has already altered all security protocols and stuns the *Übermensch* Nathan: when the next outage comes, the doors will not close, but open.

The Desire of the Other: Speciesism or Love for Machines?

The reason for this departure from his own species lies in the previous night. In the evening of the fifth day, Nathan indulges in his need for inebriation once again: eventually, alcoholism is the actual 'power outage' and thus the driving force of the narrative. Caleb takes advantage of the situation not only to manipulate the lock mechanism, but also to watch the recorded images of Nathan's female robots' process of humanization. Shocked, he watches the recordings of the psychological and physical experiments on the women. They react more and more desperately to the lab prison with their increasing cognitive and emotive faculties. There is a reason why Nathan describes Ava as a rat in a maze in his big final monolog: that he left her exactly one choice.

The images of Jasmine, Jade and the other test versions are disturbing because their 'human reaction' is not only expressed in their desperation, but also in self-mutilation as a last resort of hopelessness – only that it is light metal parts chipping and wires fraying. Moved, Caleb walks into Nathan's bedroom. There, he finds not only the unscathed models in narrow lockers, but also the still activated robot woman Kyoko. She then pulls the fake skin – it is only an inch thin – off her machine body. In doing so, she exposes her (and with that, Ava's) artificiality very explicitly once more. This doesn't make Caleb skeptical about his feelings, about loving a machine. Rather, it makes him insecure about his own humanity. As the night advances, having returned his keycard to Nathan, he cuts his forearm to experience his own organic materiality by the flow of warm, red blood. The artificial intelligences that Nathan creates in the film (and Garland with the film) seem to be out of reach of the "uncanny valley" effect: Masahiro Mori's term (2012) to describe our human discomfort when a machine *resembles us too much*.

Thus, the surveillance footage of the fifth session diegetically explains the background story of the plot, but – much more importantly – it also serves the purpose of a dramatic raising of the moral stakes. Nathan is fully aware of the fact that he is dealing with an AI, information that is repeatedly activated in his mind. He decides in favor of freeing the robots, driven by empathy and love, and against the plan of his fellow human being. In that moment, speciesism is overcome. No longer is there anything that can stop a world of machines that could as well turn against humanity – see Ava, or of course HAL 9000 in Kubrick's cult classic *2001: A Space Odyssey*. Therefore, *Ex Machina* does not only show the juxtaposition of two consecutive surveillance regimes by way of the history of media. Through human politics, it also tells the story of a possible path into technological singularity on which humanity, represented by old Adam Caleb, does what German media theorist Friedrich Kittler called the remaining three residues "dance, jazz, libido" (Kittler 1989, 536): It *desires*. This is the only path of those who do not know how to code or those – as is the case with the programmer Caleb – for whom formal language is not (or no longer) sufficient.

English translation: Patrick Ploschnitzki[4]

References

Acemoglu, Daron (2009): *Introduction to Modern Economic Growth*. Princeton, NJ: Princeton University Press.

Čapek, Karel (2004): *R.U.R. (Rossum's Universal Robots)*. [1920/1921]. London: Penguin Classics.

Kittler, Friedrich (1989): Die Welt des Symbolischen – eine Welt der Maschine. In: Großklaus, Götz/Lämmert, Eberhard (eds.): *Literatur in einer industriellen Kultur*. Stuttgart: Klett-Cotta, 521-36.

Levin, Thomas/Frohne, Ursula/Weibel, Peter (eds.) (2002): *CTRL [SPACE]. Rhetorics of Surveillance from Bentham to Big Brother*. Cambridge, MA: MIT Press

Lewis, Randolph (2017): *Under Surveillance. Being Watched in Modern America*. Austin, TX: University of Texas Press.

Mori, Masahiro (2012): The Uncanny Valley [1970]. Translated by Karl F. MacDorman and Norri Kageki. *IEEE Robotics & Automation Magazine*, June 2012, 98-100.

Müller von Blumencron, Matthias (2015): Jaron Lanier im Gespräch: Warum wollt ihr unseren Quatsch? *Frankfurter Allgemeine Zeitung*, 2 July 2015,

4 | The translation has been reworked by the author.

http://www.faz.net/aktuell/feuilleton/debatten/die-digital-debatte/internet-vordenker-jaron-lanier-im-gespraech-13679623-p4.html

Rheingold, Howard (1991): *Virtual Reality*. New York/London: Simon & Schuster.

Rid, Thomas (2016): *Maschinendämmerung. Eine kurze Geschichte der Kybernetik*. Berlin: Ullstein Buchverlage/Propyläen. [English: *Rise of the Machines: the Lost History of Cybernetics*. New York/London: W.W. Norton & Company Inc. (2016)]

Solow, Robert M. (1956): A Contribution to the Theory of Economic Growth. *The Quarterly Journal of Economics* 70, no. 1, 65-95.

Turner, Fred (2006): *From Counterculture to Cyberculture. Stewart Brand, The Whole Earth Network, and the Rise of Digital Utopianism*. Chicago, IL: Chicago University Press.

Welzer, Harald (2017): Demokratie. In: Beyes, Timon/Metelmann, Jörg/Pias, Claus (eds.): *Nach der Revolution. Ein Brevier digitaler Kulturen*. Hamburg: Edition Speersort, 187-197.

Žižek, Slavoj (1992): *Enjoy your Symptom! Jacques Lacan in Hollywood and Out*. London/New York: Routledge.

Zuboff, Shoshana (2015): Big other: surveillance capitalism and the prospects of an information society. *Journal of Information Technology* 30, 75-89.

Frankenstein's Legacy

Discursive Thinking in the Economic Paradigm

Scott Loren

Thinking revolution as a reversal in the order of things, Foucault points toward the status of literature changing in its relationship to knowledge during the nineteenth century, when it "ceased to belong to the order of discourse and became the manifestation of language in its thickness" (Foucault 1998, 265). Whereas knowledge in the Classical period was characterized by narrative continuity, with the rise of institutionalism and industrialism it was reconstituted as "a sort of general and systematic taxonomy of things" (ibid. 264). This reversal in order sets the stage for reflexive modernity as a fundamentally economic paradigm. Insofar as we can speak of social scientific functionalism in modernization processes (Habermas 1996), we might think of the economic paradigm as constituting a systemization of processes according to principles of automation, particularly in the relational dynamics of human-machine interaction (HMI). This was true for the period Foucault addresses, as it is for our present moment of conjunctural change. Mediated as it is through advances in machine learning and natural language cognition, we may be obscure witnesses to another reversal in the order of things, back toward discourse but with a difference. While discourse has reassumed a function of technologizing HMI productivity, modernity's current iteration focuses on the cultivation of language cognition patterns through the algorithmic management of HMI.

The current moment of reversal has been facilitated through the conjoined affordances of digital media convergence, inclusive network recursion, data stockpiling, user complicity and free algorithmic labor. In an expansive machine environment where traces of human presence appear as transient networks of synaptic association and loops of programmatic action, we work in conjunction with intelligent machines and infrastructures to produce resources for the real evolution of those machines and infrastructures. This peculiar reversal in HMI economies heralds a "second machine age" (Brynjolfsson and McAfee 2014). While the fact of conjunctural change in the present is tangible, and while its having something to do with the affordances noted above seems sensible, close proximity makes it difficult to perceive what the near-future contours of reflexive modernity might be. As a revolution in machine intelligence and cognitive labor, this is particularly true for its potential impact on the status of knowledge.

Following Luhmann's suggestion that an understanding of present situations might be facilitated through comparison to "older forms of descriptions of the future" (Luhmann 1998, 64), I want to read three scenes of conjunctural storytelling as a technique for screening reversals in the order of thinking things. My analysis seeks to provide a heuristic for thinking the limits of knowledge in transitional periods, and the critical role discursive cognition has played in the representation of HMI. Illustrating a particular configuration of techno-epistemic shift, each scene evidences an aesthetic of heightened self-reflexivity. Part of what makes them exceptional is their ludic character, or the way they try to trick the reader into or out of perceptual habit. They each employ a reflexive trope accompanied by a feint or ruse that fundamentally reorganizes the text's aesthetico-ideational economy once discovered. They do so with such performative acuity in their respective framing of the conjunctural moment that, more often than not, these ruses go unnoticed.

The first scene is from Mary Shelley's *Frankenstein; or, the Modern Prometheus* (1818). Against the background of Hobsbawm's Dual Revolution (Hobsbawm 2006), *Frankenstein* prototypically presents the conjuncture of industrialization technologies and institutional unrest through the trope of the *frame*. Its ruse is found in the elliptic references to the mechanical weaving frame and revolutionary frame-breaking in the Luddite uprisings. It is a period where the invention of the flying shuttle for mechanical looms revolutionized the textile-weaving industry; once the largest industry in England. With the introduction of punch-card technologies shortly after, the Jacquard loom was an important forerunner of modern computer programming, and as such an originary iteration of programmatic HMI.

The second scene is from Alan Turing's "Computing Machinery and Intelligence" (1950). Contextualized by the rise of intelligence as a cultural form following the era of "total war" (Hobsbawm 1996), and central to the emerging socio-economic logics of cold war and post-imperial military-industrial capitalism, Turing's seminal text represents the conjunctural moment through the conceptual trope of the *game*. Its ruse can be found in the ludic double inversion of deceptive imitation, where intelligent machines assume human roles and humans are programmed to function like machines.

The third scene is from Google's corporate rebranding and restructuring. The company's public announcement in 2015 hails the onset of a language-cognition driven "A.I. awakening" (Lewis-Kraus 2016), where intelligence explosion results from data-stockpile accessibility and advances in the capacities of inclusive-network computing. Turing prognosticated these conditions of a massive expansion in decentralized storage memory, processing power and the programmatic introduction of random elements that, together, might facilitate thinking in universal machines around the turn of the century. The public announcement of Google's restructuring and rebranding represents the conjunctural moment of machine intelligence Turing foresaw through the conceptual trope of *naming*. Its feint is in the deflection of attention through linguistic ambivalence, affective impulse and emotive attachments to formative moments of language acquisition.

Textuality – Shelley's Frames

Mary Shelley's *Frankenstein* is concerned with conjunctural transitions of late 18th century Europe that are integral to the economic paradigm: novel modes of societal organization (institutionalism), ideological shifts of secularization and individualism (Enlightenment humanism), the lack of social equality (slavery and emerging class society), epistemic shifts toward scientific empiricism (and German idealism), and the transition from agrarianism to industrialism. With such an abundance of novelty, a common misreading has been to understand too narrowly the scope of out-of-control technologies this story addresses. However, Shelley is careful not to address these things by aesthetic habits of exposition. Her depictions of technosocial automation are articulated by *framing* the limits of knowledge, and through what Barbara Johnson termed "explanatory ellipsis" (Johnson 2014, 6). As she suggested, Shelley's sleight of hand is not to show the reader what he is unable to see, but to show him his condition of not seeing (ibid.). This indirect reflection on technosocial transition through techniques of framing and elision is evident in the story's title.

The Modern Prometheus refers to classical mythology and the fatalistic episteme of tragedy, while bringing these into a contemporary context of early scientism through an indirect reference to Benjamin Franklin's experiments in electromagnetism. The hidden reference is made by way of Kant, who famously referred to Franklin as a *modern Prometheus* (cf. Rogers and Stevens 2012). Mobilizing the Prometheus myth in reference to Franklin provides an ideational framework of foreshadowing for diegetic character and plot development, and for thinking the extra-diegetic state of technosocial innovation as radically disruptive: as progenitor of the human race and life-giver through the originary technology of fire, Prometheus is associated with the pursuit of scientific knowledge and the consequences of obtaining it by breaking the frame of possibility. Its outward references to Prometheus and Franklin help to construct an initial frame for the eponymous narrator, Victor Frankenstein, as well as for the fact that the other narrator – Frankenstein's monster – is never named.

Ascribing Frankenstein narrative authority, the story becomes one of a young scholar from an affluent family whose demise results from the Promethean usurpation of occult knowledge and divine technology. As a student of natural philosophy who collects disparate body parts, assembling them into a super-human physical frame and animating it with the secrets of electromagnetism, Frankenstein is unambiguously depicted as a modern Promethean-Franklin. However, it is also possible to take the omission of the other main character-narrator in the story title as a gestural inclusion of that which cannot (yet) be named. Recalling Foucault's *taxonomy of things*, naming as an act of empirical order is a recurrent trope throughout, and is intelligible in Shelley's framings of genre, narrative voice and self-description.

Shelley aligns structural shifts in narrative framing with shifts in narrative voice and generic style. The story's three narrators are Robert Walton, Victor Frankenstein and the nameless creature. Walton begins the tale with a series of letters addressed to his sister: "You will rejoice to hear that no disaster has accompanied the commencement of my enterprise" (Shelley 13). While the letters function according to literary conventions of the frame narrative, opening with the letter genre also looks outward beyond the diegetic frame, providing a mirror for letter writing as a popular genre concomitant to advances in transportation technologies and the advent of mass literacy (cf. Allen 2008). The literacy, letter writing and mobility implicated by genre at this outer narrative frame also constitute crucial thematic elements in the story's development and in Shelley's reflexive ruse on communicating conjunctural change.

Following Walton's fifth letter, narrative voice shifts to Victor Frankenstein, whose autobiographical account of events is told in a confessional manner. Victor's manic admissions of glory and guilt gesture beyond the diegetic frame at Rousseau: a fellow Genevan confessionist, educational reformer and secular rationalist. Like Walton's narrative, Victor's story is a frame for the historical turn towards individualism, a point Shelley accentuates by beginning with the first-person subjective pronoun: "I am by birth a Genevese, and my family is one of the most distinguished of that republic. My ancestors had been for many years counsellors and syndics, and my father had filled several public situations with honour and reputation. He was respected by all who knew him for his integrity and indefatigable attention to public business" (Shelley 30). As David Shishido notes, Victor's autobiography reiterates the self-reflecting Hegelian subject and "divided self-consciousness" (Shishido 2011, 118) already established with Walton, but where Walton's narrative calls attention to the conventions of letter writing in the first instance, Victor's makes the new orders of class society intelligible. With his genealogical claim to authority through heritage, Victor's *I* appears to present a (Hegelian) "self-understanding of liberal society which is based on the non-selfish parts of the human personality, and seeks to preserve that part as the core of the modern political project" (Fukuyama 1992, 145). If Victor forgets his debt to society in the end, it is because he has lost the capacity to recognize his own contributions to the new world around him.

Contrasted to both Walton and Victor, the creature is singular in its total lack of heritage. With no ancestry, no name, no social context and no mirror to its sense of self, the creature occupies a position of radical alterity (cf. Loren 2004/2018). If Walton's other-directed *You* at the outermost frame represents an empathetic social sensibility, and Frankenstein's self-determined *I* represents a state of aristocratic self-awareness, embedded at the center of these is a nameless thing free of history and without specificity. This is well articulated in the creature's first words as it assumes narrative voice at the story's innermost frame: "It is with considerable difficulty that I remember the original era of my being; all the events of that period appear confused and indistinct" (Shelley 98).

Emphasizing the quality of *thingness* by beginning with the pronominal distinction *it*, the creature's self-story is one of providing things with names. As "a poor, helpless, miserable wretch" that "knew, and could distinguish, nothing" (Shelley 98), the creature's world is one of manifold lack. Here we see that the creature's lack of narrative continuity hinders temporal order, while the lack of categorical distinction disallows empirical knowledge. As such it finds itself between two spaces of negation: the obscured recollection of an irrevocable past, and an immanently unrecognizable present. With these representational parameters, Shelley gestures toward the conjunctural moment of *dual revolution*, moving from the sovereignty of the Word to that of secular institutionalism, and from the scene of the agrarian narrativity, with its chrono-logical orders, to the schematic discontinuities of industrialism. While Shelley resists conventional modes of aesthetic articulation that might allow for a simple identification of these parallel conjunctural scenes (Loren 2018), they are both formally mediated through the shared techniques of shifting narrative voice and the double-frame story. With two narrative frames outlying the *mise-en-abyme* of the creature's story, we thus have a performative gesture toward the double mediation of self at the outset of reflexive modernity. On the one hand the modern subject *appears* to be produced as a technosocial object of institutional order. On the other hand the same individual *disappears* into the nameless mass of *Lumpenproletariat* anonymity that is abstracted into a prosthetic function of industrial production (cf. Gardner 1994, Montag 2000). If the double frame narrative and shift in voice signal the dynamic compressions of *dual revolution* mediating modernity *per se* as well as the modern self, the historical lack of recognition characterizing new class relations, narrative discontinuity and alienation are symbolically inscribed in the creature's physical frame.

In(di)visible Bodies: Framing Frame-Breaking

As Bouriana Zakharieva has suggested, one of the most striking characteristics of the creature is its "composite body" (Zakharieva 1996, 416). Constructed with "materials" from the "dissecting room and the slaughterhouse" in Frankenstein's "workshop of filthy creation" (Shelley 52), this bodily frame is the symbolic site of technosocial conjuncture. In its materiality of dis-membering and re-membering, it conjoins disparate members of other bodies to create a paradox of absence in presence. The creature's remembered body thus synthesizes life and death, incorporating within it an opposition of things that allow it to accommodate an array of contradictions: "intellect and feeling; a humanist disappointment of scientific progress; the moral consequences of science probing into the secrets of life/nature and the Christian implications of this problem; the utopian visions of a new man (a new society) as a direct ideological response to the political ideas of the French Revolution, etc." (Zakharieva 1996, 741).

With the specular disjuncture of the creature's composite body, its inscrutable production in a "workshop of filthy creation", and Victor's repeated failure to recognize it as a subject in language, we can now turn to the question of visuality, mobility and industrial production relative to the creature's symbolic value through explanatory ellipsis. As Chris Baldick has argued, early receptions of *Frankenstein* read the portraiture of out-of-control technologies with the creature as an archetype of class oppression and the laboring masses. Building on Baldick's reading, Edith Gardner notes that, in addition to being "interpreted as an allegory of the French Revolution" (Gardner 1994, 71), *Frankenstein* can also be understood "as a depiction of the contemporary situation in Britain in terms of the Luddite uprisings which occurred between 1811 and 1817" (ibid. 70).

Gardner makes a compelling argument for how Shelley's writings thematically and linguistically "make reference to the Luddites" and the widespread "fear of revolution" (ibid. 70-1). The focus on discourse and failed diplomacy through language in the diegesis finds historical parallels in the textile labor movements, whose failure to gain recognition through diplomacy and discourse subsequently resulted in more radical measures that sought recognition through revolt. The repeated failures on behalf of employers and parliament to respond to petitions are striking in resemblance to the creature's pleas for recognition that remain strangely unintelligible to Victor, even when he must suffer the consequences of not taking responsibility for what he has called into the world. Gardner also points toward the historical locations of resistance. Known as "the Luddite Triangle," the uprisings were directed at framework knitting and lace trade in Nottinghamshire, Leicester and Derbyshire; the cotton trade in Lancashire and Cheshire, where industrial power looms were implemented; and at the shearing and wool industry in Yorkshire (ibid.

73). Notably, Victor's travels (taking place in the storyworld of the late 1790s) move directly through major sites of HMI commercial production, including the Luddite triangle; and yet no industry is visible.

There are thus two major sites of explanatory ellipsis intelligible in their specular and discursive occlusion. The threshold space of Victor's "workshop of filthy creation" is a proto-industrial factory where the bodily frame is automated, but whose processes and attributes are discontinuously portrayed. As Warren Montag suggests, this specular-discursive occlusion is mirrored in Victor's travels through Paris and London, and to the Lake District via Edinburgh, which presumably take him through Lower Scotland, Yorkshire and Manchester. Moving through the site of revolutionary France and what with increasing clarity was becoming the cradle of automated industry, there is no sign or mention of these. With the creature's animation, they are what Frankenstein symbolically calls into existence: "If the modern (the urban, the industrial, the proletarian) were allowed to appear, the monster would no longer be a monster... Instead, the mass is reduced to the absolute singularity of Frankenstein's creation, which is therefore not so much the sign of the proletariat as of its unrepresentability" (Montag 2000, 395).

While narrative framing techniques and the creature's bodily frame symbolically gesture at the new technologies of automated frame weaving, invisibility at these and other locations serves as a ruse in which Shelley additionally gestures toward representational failure through explanatory ellipsis. Like the creature, who – with his broken frame of a body – remains unrecognizable beyond the human detritus left in its wake, the textile workers' lack of equitable social representation becomes infamously memorable in rebellious acts of frame-breaking; a political undertaking whose symbolic value is often mistaken for material pragmatism. As if deficiencies in social diplomacy could be solved by displacing agency onto a few dumb machines. The problem is not only one of material displacement in a genealogy of automated HMI, but concomitant displacements of representation and recognition throughout the economic paradigm.

Analogy – Turing's Games

The conjunctural moment of post-industrial-scale warfare in 1950 was outwardly marked by international diplomacy and decolonization, and inwardly marked by structural transformations giving rise to a new world order. War-era decolonization led by no means to a forfeiture of infrastructural-material resources that had been set in place over the course of industrial imperialism. Acting as a conduit for the transition from New Imperialist state monopolies to post-war state capitalism, technosocial transitions in this era allow for their re-institutionalization: "Post-war capitalism was unquestionably...a 'new' version of the old system" (Hobsbawm 1996, 270). Under this dramatic double mask of diplomacy and protectionism, decentralized extensions of politico-economic power cultivated a geo-politics of Cold War espionage, surveillance and strategic deception, and are the second site of reversal in reflexive modernity's automation economies.

According to Hobsbawm, "Turing's celebrated paper of 1935, which was to provide the foundation of modern computer theory, was originally written as a speculative exploration for mathematical logicians. The war gave him and others the occasion to translate theory into the beginnings of practice for the purpose of code-breaking" (ibid. 527). Ending the era of industrial-scale warfare, military intelligence converged with machine intelligence in the use of analog-computer cyphering machines. From this point onward, the automation of mechanical computation and programmatic code would be central to transitions of the information age and knowledge economy. The shifts from total war to cold war, and decolonization to cold colonialism thus constitute a techno-epistemic shift from industrial production to computational intelligence. Published in October 1950, Turing's "Computing Machinery and Intelligence" marks these transitions in a conjunctural story of ludic deception characteristically reflexive of the technosocial moment.

Language Games: Intelligence in the Post-War Moment

Turing's very first gesture in "Computing Machinery and Intelligence" is to open a space of ambiguity: "*The Imitation Game.* I PROPOSE to consider the question, 'Can machines think?'" (Turing 1950, 433). Unlike a directly posed question, this disingenuous proposition generates issues of decidability, first implying there may be a problem with the content of the query, thus requiring consideration, and next that there may be a problem in the query's formulation, which requires further specification prior to a reflection on the query that appears to be posed. Once these issues are clarified, a consideration of the query proper might be pursued. In programmatic fashion, and with no lack of humor, Turing addresses each of these elements. *The Imitation Game* opens with a ruse on the reliability of natural language, and thus on the epistemic status of natural language cognition: the consideration "should begin with the definition of the terms 'machine' and 'think'" (ibid.). Not only is there ambiguity built into words as signs, there is also the problem of consulting the proper authority to determine the taxonomic status of these words: should meaning be provided through "a statistical survey such as the Gallop poll?" (ibid.)

Here we have an initial glimpse of the contest at hand: human thinking as lexical ambivalence and idiosyncratic association versus machine logic as statistical enquiry (into natural language cognition) to determine truth-value through majority opinion. In these opening lines, Turing has already reversed agential roles, divesting humans of their capacity for rational thought, and investing machine-computational procedures (survey calculations) with the capacity to mediate an expression of collective truth. This is precisely the function of language as a social technology: a lexical sign can be attached to a set of ideas or quasi-objects and employed with identifiable meaning insofar as its collective negotiation limits the set of associations in conventional usage. As such, Turing displaces human agency and ascribes the work of natural language processes to computational procedure.

Having nearly considered the question *Can machines think?* Turing returns to it in yet another deferral: "I shall replace the question by another, which is closely related to it and is expressed in relatively unambiguous words" (ibid.). Note here that Turing omits the substantive term that *another* should qualify, allowing his reader to fill in this lexical blank with the implied antecedent *question*: *I shall replace the question by another question*. Grammatically and idiomatically, it is a logical assumption. Having moved from the question of machine thinking to the problem of linguistic ambiguity, however, Turning does not replace the original question with another question. Capitalizing on the relative ambiguity of words, he replaces the initial *consideration*, as a problem of determinacy, with a "new form of the problem" (ibid.):

> ...the problem will be described in terms of a game we will call the 'imitation game'. It is played with three people, a man (A), a woman (B), and an interrogator (C) who may be of either sex. The interrogator stays in a room apart from the other two. The object of the game for the interrogator is to determine which of the two is the man and which is the woman. (ibid.)

A string of game parameters and sample scenarios ensue. As they develop, we find that there is not only a single objective – that of the interrogator – but also ones for the man (to trick the interrogator into thinking he is the woman and B is the man) and the woman (to help the interrogator correctly determine which is the woman and which the man). Following this implicit gesture toward the cultural codification of men as deceptive and women as supportive, Turing then introduces a third conceptual parameter in yet another return to his original query:

> We now ask the question, 'What will happen when a machine takes the part of A in this game?' Will the interrogator decide wrongly as often when the game is played like this as he does when the game is played between a man and a woman? These questions replace our original, 'Can machines think?' (ibid. 434)

At this point, the imitation game becomes recognizable as an iteration of the Turing Test. The basic goal is to test whether a computer can deceive a human into believing it is communicating with another human. As critics and proponents have argued, at stake is not a question of thinking in the conventional sense, but the tasks of imitating, deceiving, interpreting and evaluating (Warwick and Shah 2016). To what extent, then, does this *facsimile* (L. *making alike*) through *analogy* (L. *sequence of speech*) constitute valid comparability between potentially thinking yet disparate things?

Programmed as they are into the structure of his proposal, Turing anticipates such criticisms, addressing them in terms of what we mean by thinking, intelligence and intellect; by problematizing distinctions between types of machines, as well as between machines, technology and technique; between human machines, gendered machines, conceptual machine and material machines; and in particular in terms of knowledge as situated in multitudinous ways. Thus, aesthetic habits of distinction between the conceptual and the material, and between thought and action, are also generally (if implicitly) problematized. Moreover, Turing addresses the question of how significant the differences between conventional notions of thinking and imitation are for the experiment at hand. If the test is successful, what does it mean for a human to not know the nature of the entity it is communicating with? What does it mean for a machine to know how to imitate a human to the extent of being indistinguishable? Further on, Turing addresses the possibility of digital computers that can learn, make informed changes to their own programs and thus also devise innovative strategies for problem solving. He returns yet again to the original question of machine thinking, theorizing that universal computational machines would be able to evaluate a problem and generate a solution through "scientific induction" (Turing 458). Thirty years later, the first functional inductive inference program was developed by Ehud Shapiro; and Inductive Logic Programming is now a standard category for cognitive-model machine learning and logic programming.

Having opened with a language-cognition game of ambiguity, there is something like ludic wit produced between what the paper has historically achieved (its practical contribution to machine intelligence) and what it discursively displays in its performance of language games. Turing provides sites of inductive logic throughout, ranging from the broad play of lexical ambivalence and linguistic deception (for instance, where the reader assumes that *one question* will be replaced *by another question*) to the context of programmatic ludic deception: a person can or cannot guess if her interlocutor is a machine or human based on what is divinable through a series of questions and answers.

This type of ludic analogy is present in more dramatic ways as well. For example, Turing short-circuits the game to some extent early on by implying differences in the communicative and cognitive habits of men and women. Where the original distinction is implied as one between humans and machines (*Can machines think?*), splitting humans into a dual and differentiable set (men and women) impacts the range of what can be deduced as likely or possible. By subsequently switching out the man's position and replacing it with a machine, Turing partially preempts the accusation that imitating human thinking is not the same as being capable of human thinking, even if it is in some ways comparable. Now, instead of two comparable terms that might or might not be equated depending on how statistical data determines the performance of each, there are three terms, two of which are generally recognized as imbued with the capacity for thought (men and women), though the habits of language-cognition may differ between the them (Warwick and Shah 2016, 28-35). What began as a two-term equation (like or unlike) now has a third term concomitantly valorizing all possibilities: the language-cognition of women and men is both like *and* unlike. This ludic tactic impacts the parameters of possible truth-values. If human thinking can be both like and unlike itself, then a machine that appears to be like and yet is unlike a human has greater claim to validity by analogy.

Turing Complete?

There is a still more prominent analogical inversion in Turing's reflexive and performative ludism. We have seen that he subtly establishes covert double games from the beginning. This is also true for the imitation game itself, where machines imitate humans to help human cognition reflect on the possibility of machine thinking. In this *mise-en-abyme* of a game within a game, the question of a machine's capacity to perform intellectual tasks on par with human intellect becomes a question of how to qualify intellectual tasks *per se* in much the same way that, for the question of machine thinking, we must first address the question of what is meant by *machine* and *think*. From the beginning, Turing opens the double game of language-cognition ambiguity, relying on the likelihood of a lack of general consensus: incapable of agreeing on meaning, humans do not think alike regarding meanings of *thinking* and *machine*. An initial game within the game thus arises in relation to an epistemological impasse inherent in natural language cognition. However, the condition is only particular to linguistic meaning if we also assume an inextricable relation between human thought and natural language.

On one hand, the reader should agree that the problem of consensus is a real pragmatic issue when seeking to address the question of machine intelligence. Accordingly, Turing reformulates the question of machine intelligence as a problem-solving exercise with the capacity to achieve the following:

- remove ambiguity by
- introducing a set of non-ambiguous rules and commands that
- enable a scenario of interactive performance around
- the exchange of information, thus
- generating a new set of information that is
- quantifiable and has evaluative use

On the other hand, the problem of language cognition and meaning consensus is particular to the human condition and foreign to finite-state machines. Should Turing have wanted to give an example of machine intelligence as opposed to human thinking, which machines can imitate, perhaps it would have been instructive to invert the game of machines imitating humans, and have humans imitate machines to illustrate the procedural functions of machine logic. Such an illustration could suggest that difference might be one of *degrees*. As I have tried to illustrate above, this is precisely what Turing does.

The explicit meaning of *imitation* in Turing's game indicates the diegetic (game-internal) action of a computer programmed to imitate human behavior. What generally goes unnoticed by the engaged reader willing to play along with Turing's language games is the *quality* of change in his substitutions: what was initially an ambiguous language-game question becomes a programmatic empirical exercise in machine behavior. Whereas an exercise in cognitive reflection on the possibility of thinking machines may only end in an infinite regress of terminological distinction and subjective association (this is how the Turing Test conventionally functions), with the clearly structured set of variables and procedural instructions for performing tasks as part of an equation, the rules for the *imitation game* generate quantifiable results that may be evaluated and activated subsequently for further use.

If the imitation game sets parameters that frame machines doing as humans do, by turning the original question into a schematic problem with programmatic instructions and quantifiable data output, it also does the opposite: humans imitating computational programmatic logic. This type of quick-witted role reversal is characteristic of Turing's ludic discursive style: "we wish to exclude from the [category of] machines men born in the usual manner;" (Turing 435). It is perhaps no wonder that Turing's conceptual machines are programmed with similar capacities to relativize a task with a self-reflexive, self-referential style and tone that sometimes sound very much like sarcasm:

Interrogator's Question: "Please write me a sonnet on the subject of the Forth Bridge"
Answer: "Count me out on this one. I never could write poetry." (Turing 434)

From this perspective, one is tempted to wonder whether Turing, conjoining the infinite regress of natural language cognition and programmatic logic of machine intelligence, incorporates by implication a variation on his initial query: can machines have a sense of humor? Thus articulated, the question precludes the possibility that machines *cannot* think. Moreover, readers are left to consider whether it is a human or a machine generating this answer. As such, the reader is already engaged in a potential imitation game and uncertain about who speaks. If it were a machine response, as it could conceivably be, would we not assume it is able to imitate humor?

In yet another turn of ludic trickery, Turing admits that he is not really interested in posing the question *Can machines think?* For Turing, machine intelligence is a foregone conclusion; one that he claims will become evident to a broader public in the future:

> The original question, 'Can machines think?' I believe to be too meaningless to deserve discussion. Nevertheless I believe that at the end of the century the use of words and general educated opinion will have altered so much that one will be able to speak of machines thinking without expecting to be contradicted. (Turing 442)

If Turing provides a doubly recursive analogy for human intelligence via human programmability, his conceptual machinery also provides analogies for future states of human-machine interaction and epistemic shift. Taking the paper as a whole into consideration, it strikes me that "Computational Machinery" might be understood as conjunctural storytelling in its attempt to make what the author perceives to be a future episteme intelligible to the episteme of his time, even if by trickery. In this same paper, Turing narrates a fictional future of digital computing and computer processing units as interchangeable universal machines, predicting their mass dissemination and subsequent cultural naturalization; thus writing the script of our current technosocial transitions toward inclusive network computational systems.

The status of intelligence is currently being revised alongside the status of natural language as they balloon beyond the domain of human cognition. Hidden in plain sight, Turing's explication of human agency transformed into a prosthetic value of an HMI algorithm has written the rules for a conceptual experiment in which mass human agency is technologized in the production of post-anthropocentric narrative cognition. Implicit in Google's 2015 rebranding as *Alphabet* is Turing's next great feat of foresight: to have foreseen free cognitive labor as a consensual undertaking of human-machine interaction in a new order of numerical narrativity.

Digitality – Google's Names

On August 10, 2015, Google announced plans to create the holding company Alphabet Incorporated. Explaining the company's motives in the official blog "G Is For Google," co-founder and CEO Larry Page comments on name choice: "We liked the name Alphabet because it means a collection of letters that represent language, one of humanity's most important innovations, and is the core of how we index with Google Search! We also like that it means alpha-bet (Alpha is investment return above benchmark), which we strive for!" (Google Inc. 2015). Corporate branding, as we know, entails the creation of signs that become imbued with meaning, allowing the public to identify a company and its products, and to establish a collection of associations. By commenting on what is attractive about the brand name *Alphabet*, the blog's readership is already being urged to associate Google's new parent company with notions of language, humanity, innovation and capital growth. While this seems a logical tactic, the gestural relation to specificities of the technosocial moment is oddly, if somewhat obviously, negotiated.

Facile answers to the question of why to restructure and rebrand in 2015 are evident in the blog announcement and reiterated in news media, where priority was given to creating financial and managerial transparency. As for the name, Alphabet is pre-coded with useful associations: it familiarly signifies innocence, possibility, ingenuity, knowledge and community. Tactically speaking, the establishment of Alphabet enables Google to maintain brand identity for its core businesses, and at the same time to dissociate from these where useful. Google's restructuring and rebranding thus also marks a shift in the company's history, allowing us to reflect on how it perceives its own temporality. Read through the lens of conjunctural storytelling, rebranding reflects shifts in the status of discursive knowledge at a specific moment of technosocial transition, where the creation of economic value coincides in new ways with the creation of discursive value.

Rethinking Click Linking

Established in 1996 by Stanford University graduate students Larry Page and Sergey Brin and incorporated two years later, Google has played a major role in the revolutionary transformation of numerous economies (financial, social, political, etc.) through its reorganization of information economies. While we continue to think of the current techno-epistemic moment in terms of the information age, characterized by digital information and communication technologies, it is the algorithm – a medium for organizing information, intention and action – that makes information intelligible and gives it specific value. Algorithms constitute the substratum of economic routine; they bend to them our cognitive habits and enfold discursive practices. Algorithms act across the exogenous landscapes humans and machines move in and co-inhabit. They are the native language and logic of the media ecologies through which cognition and communication take place. Plotting and structuring technosocial trajectories of the present, algorithms redistribute prior distributions of the sensible, and they will determine technosocial change in the future beyond what is now comprehensible. When compelled to place a finger on the period's defining moment of departure, many will point to the PageRank (PR) algorithm that grew out of the Stanford Digital Library project.

Originally intended for archiving and indexing the entirety of human knowledge on textual record, the PR algorithm was a crucial turn in the automation of cognitive inquiry. In its partial extensions of Foucault's *thick textuality* and the empirical logic of cross-referential citation, PR's indexing function significantly improved automated search techniques in Google's moment of ascension by narrowing the scope of relevant associations. Mediated by the PR algorithm, the associative linking between search terms and knowledge sites has been central to effective algorithmic labor and, thus, company success.

Twenty years ago, the brand name Google signaled a future where numeric computation would structure a brave new informational economy of individualized advertising in e-commerce. Now, the brand name Alphabet suggests a future where the signifying, associative processes that characterize natural language cognition will structure the new knowledge economy of language based research and development; an economy where not only humans are intelligent. As stated in the company's 2017 fiscal report, revenues are still generated "primarily by delivering both performance advertising and brand advertising" (Alphabet 2017, 4). However, the same competitive advantages that have allowed Google "to dominate the online advertising industry" (Jurevicius 2018) are now allowing Alphabet to lead the intelligence race: "Across the company, machine learning and artificial intelligence (AI) are increasingly driving many of our latest innovations" (Alphabet 3). The status of algorithmic work has not diminished for Alphabet, but it has changed. Its import for Google's breakthrough to market dominance in search technologies, their undisputed command of e-commerce and economic influence through advertising technologies, and their continued access to and generation of pattern-behavior user habit as an essential resource are directly relative to algorithmic labor in current human-machine interaction. The difference, as noted, is in the status of language-based knowledge, which has rapidly transitioned from a (significant) surplus value automatically generated through core practices, to a most precious resource relative to where the company is steering core developments.

Understanding Your Context

In a 2014 TED talk, Page reflected on Google's original mission to "organize the world's information and make it universally accessible" (Page/Rose 2014), comparing it to a newer vision of strategic development: "computing is kind of a mess. Your computer doesn't know where you are, it doesn't know what you're doing, it doesn't know what you know. And a lot of what we try to do recently is just make your devices work, make them understand your context – Google Now knows where you are, knows what you might need. So really I think computing, where it can understand you and understand that information – we really haven't done that yet" (ibid.) Elements of Turing's conjunctural storytelling carry over here. First, the question of human cognitive habit is minimally veiled as a placeholder for considering the future of machine intelligence. Next, a strategy of rhetorical deflection and deception is evident: in 2014, your computer knew very well where you were and what you might need (or want). These were the company's core competencies. Smart algorithms were programmed to recognize, categorize and dynamically archive patterns of language cognition left as traces in the ether. As such, HMI communication and natural language (re)cognition are equally at stake here. But if this string of deceptive claims is a feint, there is nothing false in the question of helping machines to "understand your context".

While machine intelligence has been a core competence and focus from the beginning, the company interests were invested in significantly different ways previous to the current machine-learning boom. The recent development of Neural Turing Machines and Recurrent Neural Networks marks a reorganization of computational knowledge cultures; and as machines make leaps in natural language cognition, they are increasingly responsible for high-level decision-making processes and task execution. Smart machines now enjoy degrees of autonomy that were unimaginable a few years ago. Whatever assumptions are made about value in current HMI data economies, if they are not understood as a resource for advances in machine learning, the assumption is amiss.

Fifteen months after Google announced plans to create the holding company Alphabet Incorporated, *The New York Times* ran an article announcing the "Great A.I. Awakening" (Lewis-Kraus 2016). According to the author, the advanced technologies in machine learning that had transformed Alphabet's language services platform were now "poised to reinvent computing itself" (ibid.). Here we glimpse the meaning of *Alphabet* that was implicit all along, but subordinated under the other logics of nominal distinction. If the exclamatory fervor of the *Times* piece has a touch of belatedness, a circular logic is also implicit in its central claim. With Translate as an intelligence-driven platform, and with the current state of computational technology underwritten by task-specific programing for data processing *qua* automated reasoning (i.e. algorithms), the logic might be read as follows: *machine intelligence has transformed itself and will reinvent itself.* But this is the point.

On the one hand, systemic reflexivity as a transformative operation is at stake. Human activity constitutes an important part of HMI computational logic and algorithmic labor, though human users are to be associated with *process* in the production of value this time round; not necessarily with its *telos* in the first instance, as the case was with e-commerce advertising technologies (Google's AdWords and AdSense). On the other hand, these transformative-reflexive operations generate resources that are only secondarily intelligible for humans: through the dramatically improved accuracy of Google's translation services as of mid- to late 2016, for example. Not only do intelligent machines understand the contexts of where you are and what you want; they can now communicate for you what you think you might like to say in a language whose cognitive patterns of symbolic association remain completely foreign to you. Greetings to John Searle from the Chinese room: the fundamental point in present technosocial transition is not the programmatic capacity for choosing a proper character set to produce an accurate iteration of natural language use. Searle's argument was that this could be achieved without proper command or 'knowledge' of the language (cf. Searle 1980). Accurate translation is a symptom, not a cause. If the *mise-en-scène* of current HMI intelligence is neural-network machine learning that reads and interprets patterns of anthropomorphic associative behavior, then its *mise-en-abyme* is natural language cognition and the ambiguity of words.

In the current reversal of economic order, value creation is achieved through HMI's automated capacity to produce narrativity. But with more than consumer goods and monetary gain at stake, the question of purpose is a question of perspective. Depending on the locus of intended agency (human or machine), emphasis in the *telos* of human use can be placed either on the consumption of information or on its production via consumption. If the popular notion of prosumerism is a consumer that assumes a producer role in hyper-fragmented market economies, with the purpose of consuming that which it produces, this is one indication of how inadequate our understandings of human capital and surplus value have been in the current era of HMI labor. The fact that consumers can configure their own computers, design their own clothes or market their own wares on the very platforms on which they consume may be interesting as an articulation of innovative market fragmentation. However, this mistakes the ability to set the table at which one eats for the inclusive processes of producing, preparing, consuming, digesting, discharging and repurposing what is eaten. While memory traces of natural language cognition are a precious resource in the HMI production of value, the trajectory of value creation extends significantly beyond the conventions of economic efficacy in digital commerce, and even beyond finance as an iteration of economic modernity.

The value of human capital in the present might be compared to its value in the era with which we began; where the creation of class society is accompanied by a value-economy model of human capital oriented toward productive labor power. In network society, human capital is once again a highly valuable resource; particularly in its capacity as an operator interacting with machines for mass production. We have thus uncannily returned to the era of early industrialism, but instead of leaving the home for the factory, we have taken the factory home as a constant companion.

In seeking to make intelligible a genealogical countermemory inscribed in these conjunctural scenes of technosocial transition, my intention has been to historicize cognitive and representational economies in our present moment. Each of these conjunctural tales gravitates toward the shared master plot of HMI automation in economic modernity and the subplot of natural language cognition as a proto-technology that, in a double reversal, identifies human specificity only to undercut it in a subsequent turn of thought. With the shared techniques of diegetic framing, feigned closure and discordant narration, these tales perform in some capacity the epistemic shift Foucault identifies as a departure from narrativity: a departure that engenders space for the new man of enlightenment humanism, only to evacuate the same space of being in the very next instance for lack of continuity. This duality and its historical conditions of impasse have typified thought on reflexive modernity.

Characterizing modernity as the "unprecedented amalgam of new practices and institutional forms (science, technology, industrial production, urbanization); of new ways of living (individualism, secularization, instrumental rationality); and of new forms of malaise (alienation, meaningless, a sense of impending social dissolution)", Charles Taylor claimed that the central problem in the empirical study of modernity "has from the beginning been modernity itself" (Taylor 2004). In a manner recalling Shelley and her progeny of disparate identities, Taylor points to the condition of detracted conjuncture as producing "multiple modernities" that "need to be understood in terms of divergent social imaginaries involved" (ibid.). He explains, however, that social imaginaries are not constituted through a set of abstract ideas. In their institutional-like technicity, social imaginaries are "what enables, through making sense of, the practices of society" (ibid.). With real pragmatic sense-making as the affordance *par excellence* of contemporary technosocial practice, algorithmic agency assumes a place of prominence in the current social imaginary, where disparate modernities converge in novel self-understandings of narrative recursion.

References

Allen, Graham (2008): *Shelley's* Frankenstein. London and New York: Continuum, 2008.

Alphabet, Inc. (2017): Form 10-K for the Fiscal Year Ended December 31, 2017. https://www.sec.gov/Archives/edgar/data/1652044/0001652044 18000007/goog10-kq42017.htm

Baldick, Chris (1987): *In Frankenstein's Shadow.* Oxford: Clarendon Press.

Brynjolfsson, Erik/McAfee, Andrew (2014): *The Second Machine Age: Work, Progress, and Prosperity in a Time of Brilliant Technologies*. New York: W.W. Norton & Company.

Foucault, Michel (1998): *Aesthetics, Method and Epistemology*. Trans. Robert Hurley et al. Ed. James D. Faubian. New York: The New Press.

Fukuyama, Francis (1992): *The End of History and the Last Man*. New York: Free Press.

Gardner, Edith (1994): Revolutionary Readings: Mary Shelley's *Frankenstein* and the Luddite Uprisings. *Iowa Journal of Cultural Studies* 13, 70-91.

Google Inc. (2015): G is for Google. *Google Official Blog*, 10 August 2015, http://googleblog.blogspot.ch/2015/08/google-alphabet.html

Habermas, Jürgen (1996): *The Philosophical Discourse on Modernity*. Trans. Frederick G. Lawrence. Cambridge, MA: MIT Press.

Hobsbawm, Eric (2006): *The Age of Revolution 1789-1848*. London: Abacus.

Hobsbawm, Eric (1996): *The Age of Extremes 1914-1991*. New York: Vintage Books.

Johnson, Barbara (2014): *A Life with Mary Shelley*. Stanford, CA: Stanford University Press.

Jurevicius, Ovidijus (2018): SWOT analysis of Alphabet (Google). *Strategic Management Insight*, 17 April 2018, https://www.strategicmanagementinsight.com/swot-analyses/google-swot-analysis.html

Lewis-Kraus, Gideon (2016): Great A.I. Awakening. *The New York Times Magazine*, 14 December 2016, https://www.nytimes.com/2016/12/14/magazine/the-great-ai-awakening.html

Loren, Scott (2004): What are the implications of the virtual for the human? *European Journal of American Culture* 23 (3), 173-185.

Loren, Scott (2018): Words as Witness: Remembering the Present in Mary Shelley's *Frankenstein*. *SPELL Swiss Papers in Literature and Language* 36, 67-100.

Luhmann, Niklas (1998): *Observations on Modernity*. Stanford, CA: Stanford University Press.

Montag, Warren (2000): The Workshop of Filthy Creation: A Marxist Reading of *Frankenstein*. *Mary Shelley's Frankenstein: A Case Study in Contemporary Criticism*. Ed. Ross C. Murfin and Johanna Smith. New York: St. Martin's Press, 384-395.

Page, Larry/Rose, Charlie (2014): Larry Page at TED2014: Where's Google going next? https://www.ted.com/talks/larry_page_where_s_google_going_next

Rogers, Brett/Stevens, Benjamin (2012): Classical Receptions in Science Fiction. *Classical Receptions Journal* 4, no. 1, 127-47.

Searle, John (1980): Minds, Brains, and Programs. *The Behavioral and Brain Sciences* 3, no. 3, 417-24.

Shelley, Mary (1994): *Frankenstein*. London: Penguin Books.

Shishido, David (2011): Apotheosis Now: A Hegelian Dialectical Analysis of Mary Shelley's Frankenstein. *Berkeley Undergraduate Journal* 24, no. 3, 111-26.

Taylor, Charles (2004): *Modern Social Imaginaries*. Durham and London: Duke University Press.

Turing, Alan (1950): Computing Machinery and Intelligence. *Mind* 59, no. 236, 433-60.

Warwick, Kevin/Shah, Huma (2016): *Turing's Imitation Game: Conversations with the Unknown*. Cambridge: Cambridge University Press.

Zakharieva, Bouriana (1996): Frankenstein of the Nineties: The Composite Body. *Canadian Review of Comparative Literature* 23, no. 3, 739-52.

Bankrupt Worlds

Economic Catastrophes in the Theater of Friedrich Dürrenmatt

Daniel Cuonz

For the time being, it seems, we have made it through the worst of it. The worldwide financial crisis that began in 2007 with a collapse of the subprime mortgage market in the United States and that reached one low point after the other in the following years has not yet been overcome, and its impact is enormous, but the worst fears have fortunately not come true. Nevertheless, the temporary apocalyptic undertone in public discourse on this matter was and remains striking. The debate was haunted by a concept that first appeared in those spheres of the world wide web that are particularly prone to conspiracy theories, later, disturbingly, in the comments columns of serious newspapers, and eventually on the title page of the *Spiegel*[1] – world bankruptcy!

This notion gives an adequate impression of the diffuse fears that circulated throughout the months when the financial crisis was at its peak. Its rhetorical vividness is inversely proportional to its semantic transparency: Who goes bankrupt when the world goes bankrupt? Who would be the agents of its execution? How would they proceed? And who knows? Perhaps they are already at work, behind the stage at which we are all still staring and on which the all too real actors of high finance are still performing the ever-same comedy. And what would come after a world

1 | The headline was: "Is the World going bankrupt? US National Debt, Euro-Crisis, Market Turmoil". The cover shows two burning paper planes, one made of a dollar bill, the other made of a euro bill.

bankruptcy? Are there scenarios for something new or are we all busy rehearsing our part for a final act whose dramaturgy is yet unknown?

Dramaturgical Thinking

Even if one asks these questions in a less suggestive way, it is evident that the notion of world bankruptcy does not only address financial matters – maybe less than we would wish. And if its use in public debates was to some extent also meant as a provocation, then it does not only appeal to economic model building and political crisis management, but also to what the great 20th-century Swiss playwright Friedrich Dürrenmatt has on various occasions referred to as "dramaturgical thinking" (cf. Rüedi 2011, 519-22). Dürrenmatt's writing and thinking are of interest in this context not only because at least two of his plays anticipate scenarios that became only all too real on the world stage in the course of the financial crisis of 2008. Moreover, these plays strikingly clearly illustrate what is at stake in the notion of world bankruptcy.[2]

Dürrenmatt, as far as I can see, never used the notion of world bankruptcy himself. But one can assume that its appearance in the context of a public debate over a worldwide financial crisis would have been of interest to him. Dürrenmatt, as is well known, used to consider things from their outcome – not from any outcome, but exclusively from the worst catastrophic ending imaginable. The relevant keywords are omnipresent in his own writings as well as in the academic literature: accident, catastrophe, endgame, supernova, apocalypse, *Weltuntergang* (cf. Weber 2003).

Above all in his plays, but also in parts of his prose and in his paintings, Dürrenmatt repeatedly treats the issue of the unlikely but possible event of a crisis turning into a catastrophe. In other words, he creates aesthetic scenarios of everything that is still ahead of all those who think they have made it through the worst of it. Yet, Dürrenmatt does not only enact such scenarios, but also – and with growing interest – he considers the mental process of finding such scenarios. It is not for nothing that the last volume of his collected conversations and interviews bears the title *Dra-*

2 | Some of the following reflections, although in a different arrangement and in a larger scope, are treated in my book *Die Sprache des verschuldeten Menschen* (Cuonz 2018, 303-26).

maturgie des Denkens (*Dramaturgy of Thinking*). At one point, Dürrenmatt explicitly elaborates on this concept:

> Ladies and gentlemen, I think dramaturgically. That is, my intellectual method as a dramatist consists in transforming the social reality of man into theater, and then using this transformed reality to investigate matters further. By playing out the world, I think the world through. The result of this thought process is not a new reality, but a comedic entity in which reality encounters itself in analyzed form, or more precisely, in which the audience encounters itself in analyzed form. This analysis is governed by imagination, by experimental thought, by playfulness; so it is not strictly scientific, it is in many ways frivolous, but useful precisely for that reason. (Dürrenmatt 2006, III, 193)

What Dürrenmatt called "dramaturgical thinking" could be characterized as an ongoing process of raising awareness of the fact that the limits of a particular form of representation do not set the limits for the possibilities to deal with the problems being represented. For obvious reasons, this form of thinking is of particular importance when it comes to the outline of encounters with an unknown, but possible future, with events of whose escalation we have no historical experience: a nuclear war, a climate catastrophe – or a world bankruptcy.

The term used in this context in political, economic or technological risk analysis originates in the field of dramaturgy: "scenario planning". Hermann Kahn, one of the pioneers of this method, coined a formula that could just as well be a motto of Dürrenmatt's collected writings on drama and theater: "Thinking about the unthinkable" (Kahn 1962, cf. Horn 2014). It is Dürrenmatt's undeniable merit to have brought to light the analytical potential of considering the conceptual roots of what Kahn and others have called scenario planning, that is to say, a way of thinking trained by the consideration of the limits and possibilities the literary form of drama.

The consideration of economic scenarios with catastrophic outcomes, however, has remained marginal in Dürrenmatt research. On the one hand this seems surprising, given the fact that financial crisis situations are among the thematic elements that appear comparably often in his plays. On the other hand, an analysis based on the conventional forms of the critique of capitalism can do very little here because in Dürrenmatt's view, capitalism "is not a system, but the expression of human nature"

Dürrenmatt 1996, III, 241). This might be the reason why representations of financial crisis situations in his plays evoke a sense of alarm whose implications reach far beyond the field of economy.

In order to further illustrate the questions at stake here, it may be useful to first have a look at one of Dürrenmatt's paintings. It is entitled: "The Last General Assembly of the Federal Banking Establishment".[3] In the middle ground, the painting shows elegantly dressed gentlemen sitting at a festively laid table and holding guns pointed at themselves, whereas the equally elegantly dressed gentlemen in the fore- and background, lying on the floor and hanging on chandeliers, obviously have already killed themselves. At second glance, one recognizes the iconographic logic of this crude joke. One could refer to it as a fusion of two biblical closing tableaux. With regard to the iconographic allusions in the center of the picture and not least to its title, Dürrenmatt clearly relates his "Last General Assembly" to "The Last Supper". However, the use of color and brushstroke, the flickering reddish orange in the background and the contrasting black of the figures, evoke the scenery of the apocalypse. Within a relatively confined space and in an only all too profane setting, this painting connects hope of salvation to predictions of the end of the world, and thus indicates the basic tension in Dürrenmatt's thinking and writing as *sub specie finis*.

It is against this background that Dürrenmatt himself repeatedly pointed to the fact that he regarded his comedies as a modern "Theater of the World" (Dürrenmatt 1998, X, 133). The problem of the modern age, however, is that there can be no divine director anymore who distributes the parts and determines the plot, as in Calderon's *Gran teatro del mundo* (1655). What Dürrenmatt was interested in were the questions arising from this problem: What dramaturgic patterns of order can replace divine direction? And what patterns of disorder? How do world endgames function, when they have to refrain from the dramaturgy of punishment and reward for sin and virtue respectively?

It is certainly no coincidence that Dürrenmatt visualized these questions in the form of a painting that shows a crude joke at the expense of the world of high finance. There is reason to believe that he considered

---

3 | *Letzte Generalversammlung der Eidgenössischen Bankanstalt* (1966), oil on canvas, 72 x 60 cm, Centre Dürrenmatt, Neuchâtel.

the economic catastrophe as the most accurate setting for scenarios of a modern world endgame.

The dramaturgical principle of this modern theater of the world could be characterized by what the French philosopher Jean-Pierre Dupuy has termed *"catastrophisme éclairé"*, that is to say, the constant awareness of the fact that the worst case is a real possibility (Dupuy 2014). In Dürrenmatt's version, however, this "enlightened catastrophism" always has one more dimension. It might be said that only apocalypticists are reliable prognosticators (Sloterdijk 2010). But in Dürrenmatt, only comedians are reliable apocalypticists.

Dramaturgy of the Financial Crisis – *Romulus the Great*

Among all of Dürrenmatt's plays, *Romulus the Great*, first staged in 1947, is the one that most explicitly reflects this standpoint. And it is in this play that Dürrenmatt stages his first financial crisis: a large-scale state bankruptcy. Its theme is nothing less than the collapse of the Western Roman Empire, which in Dürrenmatt's version is due to financial factors, and, therefore, appears comic.

Romulus in any case seems determined to do everything in order to make life at his court look ridiculous. Therefore, all the laughs in acts one and two are at the expense of those who do not want to accept the profane reasons for the imminent collapse of the empire, who try to fight its obvious inevitability with awkward heroism or who copiously lament on its circumstances. In one scene, there is an insightful argument between Romulus and Zeno, the emperor of the Eastern Roman Empire, that is initiated by the appeal to Romulus to finally take the measures in order to prevent "the end of the world":

> ROMULUS. It will be the end of us. There's a big difference.
>
> ZENO. We are the world.
>
> ROMULUS. We are provincials, surrounded by a world that is growing over our heads, a world we cannot comprehend. (Dürrenmatt 2006 I, 147)

The helpless activism and the sententious chatter of Romulus' entourage stand in comic contrast to the cheerful idleness of the last Roman Emperor himself. At first, this is certainly amusing, but after a while it begins to feel unpleasant in a way that is eventually put into words by one of the characters: “A world goes up in flames and you are cracking jokes” (ibid., 107).

Indeed, the number of punchlines in the first two acts is quite high. In his review of the play, Max Frisch spoke of *Witzelei* (wisecracking), which Dürrenmatt, given his undisputable *Witz* (wit), did actually not need (Frisch 1980, 145). This is a misunderstanding. For in this play, even the most foreseeable puns and the most overused gags have an overriding importance. They indicate the inevitable inappropriateness of all activism in the face of an imminent disaster. One understands why Dürrenmatt emphasized the fact that the biggest challenge in playing the part of Romulus is to make sure that the audience does not sympathize with him all too soon (Dürrenmatt 1998, II, 120). By no means ought the spectators to mistake the cheerful bankrupt for a cynical apocalyptic jester. Rather, they have to be confronted with the question whether there is a connection between a comedic attitude and “enlightened catastrophism”.

Only when this question is posed can it come to light that Romulus is *not* the comedian for whom he is mistaken by everyone. He is just playing him. He neither underestimates nor ignores the seriousness of the situation. But he sees it differently than the others. It is his conviction that world empires inevitably become guilty vis-à-vis the world community – the more powerful they become and the longer they exist, the heavier weighs their guilt. Romulus' demonstrative passivity conceals a long-term calculation of action that is revealed in act 3 on the occasion of a dialogue between the emperor and his wife:

> JULIA. Right from the start you had nothing else in mind except bringing about the fall of Rome.
> ROMULUS. Nothing else.
> JULIA. You consciously sabotaged the rescue of the Empire?
> ROMULUS. Consciously.
> JULIA. You played the cynic and the gluttonous buffoon, just to stab us in the back.ROMULUS. You could put it that way.
> JULIA. You deceived me.
> ROMULUS. You deceived yourself about me. You assumed I was just as power-hungry as you. You were calculating, but your calculation was wrong.
> JULIA. Your calculation is right.
> ROMULUS. Rome is falling. Julia. You are Rome's traitor.
> ROMULUS. No, I am Rome's judge. (Dürrenmatt 2006, I, 166)

What is striking in this key passage is the insistent vocabulary of calculation that points to the logic of action, which regulates the playacting of the *incognito* judge of the world. It is a dramaturgy of bankruptcy. Romulus plots to lead the Roman Empire's economy to a point that its morality reached a long time ago. What he tries to correct is the scandalous fact that there is generally no inner connection between the guilt of an empire and its decline. With the "bankruptcy of the Roman empire" (ibid., 133), which he actively promotes, Romulus tries to close a gap of plausibility in the process of world history. If his plan succeeded, the over-indebtedness of the Roman Empire would stand in a relation of analogy to its guilt and in a relation of causality to its punishment

The logic of this plot is gradually and playfully conveyed to the audience by means of a wide variety of linguistic jokes and scenic ideas. A particularly engaging scene is the appearance of a super-rich manufacturer of trousers. His name reveals his mission: Cäsar Rupf (Caesar Pluck) seeks to restore the old dignity of a world empire that has literally degenerated into a chicken yard. In the jargonized self-important language of the newly rich man of affairs, he lets the emperor know that he not only has the means to instantly fix the empire's financial problems, but also to move the Teutons to vacate Roman territory – in the sense of an investment, of course, that is to say, of a fusion between a world empire and a global company. With this, the capitalist becomes a useful idiot for the self-proclaimed judge of the world: Romulus just has to turn into a catchphrase what Rupf's offer reveals: "The fatherland can only be saved with money, or it will surely be lost. We must choose between a catastrophic capitalism and a capital catastrophe" (ibid., 167).

With that said, the comedy of debt has reached the point at which its initiator can reveal it to be the exposition of a heroic redemption of guilt. However, Romulus has miscalculated on his part, as, when the Teutons finally arrive, their leader Odoaker turns out to be an overly human contemporary. He does not even think about killing Romulus; on the contrary, he seeks to prevent one cruel world empire from immediately being replaced by another. All that Romulus can do now is to accept his part in this perpetual endgame: "Let's do it quickly. Let's do a comedy one last time. Let us act as if a balance could really be struck here on earth [...]" (ibid., 186). And, thus, Romulus and Odoaker play the comedy of the conquest of Rome by the Teutons and give to an unexpected catastrophe that certain semblance of meaning that only comedians are able to wring from an otherwise meaningless reality.

The option of an ultimate, all-embracing act of sense-making, however, has become obsolete. Now Romulus *is* the fool he thought he had just played – locked up in his own plot with no way out into a real world that would be meaningfully shapeable in any kind of way. What Odoaker and Romulus painfully learn from each other is that reality is itself a comedy. A comedy, however, in which no one knows what part he will have played in it.

The moral and economic juncture with which Romulus tried to bridge a causality gap in world history has not withstood the strain of reality. The obsolence of Romulus' ethical strategy has its dramaturgic equivalent in the self-imprisonment of his all too targeted comedic play-acting, or, to put it more technically, in the non-transformability of a comedy of debt into a scenario of moral redemption.

Too Big to Fail or: Worse Than the "Worst Turn" – *Frank V*

This insight constitutes the central challenge for the further development of Dürrenmatt's concept of comedy. And it is certainly no coincidence that one of the most important new approaches in his theatrical thinking was tested in a play that stages the dramaturgy of financial crisis within the thematic framework of its representative institution: *Frank V. Comedy of a Private Bank*. In a statement published on the occasion of the first book edition of this play, Dürrenmatt commented on this development as follows:

> The course I have taken with my theater cannot be understood without further ado. Without dropping the comic and playfulness as its means, it has made the transition from "thinking about the World" to "thinking of worlds". [...] *Frank V* can be understood in this direction, not as an economic play (it would be too naïve and too superficial for that), but as work on a feigned model. Model of what? Of possible human relations." (Dürrenmatt 1998, VI, 155)

The stage set for this world model is a bank. To be more precise: "a bank of gangsters" (Dürrenmatt 1998, VI, 186), as Dürrenmatt puts it, one, however, that faces liquidation due to its downright grotesque mismanagement. And, of course, all possible measures are taken in order to execute this liquidation as fraudulently as possible. Yet, this play is more than just an anti-capitalist knee-slapper. The aim of Dürrenmatt's new theatrical approach is not to provide a critical representation of an existing world, no matter how grotesquely misled this world might be, but rather the theatrical construction of a world model that sheds light on aspects of a given reality, which remain unnoticed in its immediate representation.

Against this background, it becomes clear why Dürrenmatt has set this play of all plays as an opera. The juxtaposition of singing and speech provides an ideal framework for the theatrical realization of its underlying idea. On the one hand, there are the business practices of the gangster bankers, presented in prose and without music: deception, disguise, dissimulation, in brief, a virtuous repertoire of formal elements of comedy, bluntly subjected to criminal abuse. But there is yet another comedy, the in-house one, so to speak, that the gangster bankers mostly perform for each other and that is exclusively presented in songs. The often drawn comparison to Brecht's *Threepenny Opera*, however is as misleading as can be. Dürrenmatt himself vehemently rejected it: "In *Frank V* people sing when they are lying – in the *Threepenny Opera*, when they are telling the truth" (Dürrenmatt 1996, I, 120).

And basically, the staff of Frank's Private Bank, although with thematic variation and changing formations, chant the ever-same lie. At one point it is made explicit by the whole staff in unison. "*Möchten Gutes tun. Doch eben. / Wollen wir im Wohlstand leben / Müssen wir Geschäfte machen*" (Dürrenmatt 1998, VI, 25). They do not want to be bad people, but in *this* world, they have no other choice.

The scandal here is not the obvious discrepancy between the vocal praise for the true, good and beautiful on the one hand and the crude daily business of the gangster bankers on the other. Not that they sing about one thing and do another. What is more problematic is that they sing about one thing in order to justify the fact that they do not do another. Therefore, the hypocritical roundel of moral relativization is at its peak and turning point when one of the characters articulates its principle: "In every hour we could have turned around, in every moment of our evil lives. There is no inheritance that could not have been declined and no crime that had to be committed" (ibid., 92). These are the words of senior clerk Böckmann, who, in the hour of his death, wants to escape from the hypocritical comedy and confess his guilt. He hopes for grace and asks for spiritual aid – but that would be too much of a risk for a bank of gangsters amidst the process of its fraudulent liquidation. Ottilie Frank, the bank director's wife in person, gives the all too insightful senior clerk the lethal injection.

And Frank V sings to it. He even accompanies the death agony of his oldest friend with a tune whose banally rhymed sing-song adheres to a false humanism that is revealed as a hopelessly bad comedy through its confrontation with the insight of a dying man. In this sense, the Böckmann scene also helps to make sense of the ending of the play. The final scene shows a collective that has failed with its all too dilettante performance of an all too transparently plotted comedy of bankruptcy.

Ironically, the ones who finally thwart Frank's plans for a fraudulent liquidation of the bank of his ancestors are his children: his son Herbert, who has a degree in economics from Oxford, and his daughter Franziska, who was educated in a fancy private school for upper-class girls in Montreux. At the very moment when the old warhorses of gangster banking come together for a comedic endgame, equipped with submachine guns and provisions for several days, deeply distrusting and thus grotesquely beleaguering each other in the strong room, they are replaced in the director's office by the young and smart pragmatics of the next generation. They have realized that it is much more effective to use the criminal potential of the existing social order than to fight it with the methods of their ancestors.

Along with this goes the fact that the seed capital for the era of Frank VI comes from the state bank. Ottilie Frank, who belatedly but all the more radically seeks revenge, asks her old school friend, the state president, to destroy the bank of her ancestors that has gone bankrupt in many senses of the word. Without success: "If you had some hundreds of millions less in debt and two dozen murders less on your conscience, then we could discuss" (ibid., 122). But since things are as they are, even the state president eventually warbles a little song by which he explains to the love of his youth that from a certain point on, it is better to no longer bother about guilt and to let the state pay for the debts.

This ridiculously brief appearance is all that is granted to the representative of the state. The concluding statements are reserved for others, for example the personnel manager of the bank, who has already had the first word in the play. This is significant, since the staff may change and the methods may be adapted to the circumstances, but, basically, everything remains the same – or is subject to eternal recurrence. The last stage direction of the play is: "All performers enter and come to the forestage" (ibid., 129). Before the curtain falls, they are all back – and they sing yet again. One will not have to wait all too long for the next crisis. Nothing is as ridiculous (and hence as dangerous) as a world that believes it has made it through the worst of it. The apocalyptic tinge of Dürrenmatt's dramaturgical thinking is never as clear as it is by the end of his banking comedy – and never was it more accurate in its prognostics.

At this point, if not before, one begins to think of Dürrenmatt's most famous contribution to literary theory: "A story is not finished until it has taken the worst turn" (Dürrenmatt 1998, VII, 7). The sentence was coined a few years after the first staging of *Frank V.* But it seems that it undercuts the dramaturgical radicalism that Dürrenmatt had already reached with his banking comedy. For the "worst turn", at least, is still a turn, that is to say, the logical final step of a given scenario. The scenario of the "comedy of a private bank", however, is ostentatiously not thought through to completion. Its non-ending surrenders to the dramaturgical complexity of redemption in both the moral and the financial sense. Thus the question arises whether the dramaturgy of bankruptcy, staged in the framework of its institutional homeland, necessarily has to turn into a declaration of dramaturgical bankruptcy.

Beyond the Comedy of Financial Capitalism

Interestingly enough, this very question is explicitly raised on stage. In one of the first scenes, senior clerk Paul Böckmann steps before the curtain and articulates the dramaturgical logic of what is shown on stage. He is mandated to introduce the audience in a generally understandable way to the business practices of a bank of gangsters. And he struggles with this task in highly significant way:

> The daily business of a financial institute like ours can hardly be demonstrated, at most it can be suggested. What is most important and decisive happens in secrecy. The struggle is knotty, confusing and cruel. […] You will, therefore, probably be thankful, if we do not bother you too much with technical details, but rather speak about our human sorrows and conflicts in a more general way. It would certainly be quite beneficial for your economic education – if I may say so – to see something completely different, that is to say, to witness our truly sophisticated, ingenious business practices. But alas, we are subject to certain dramaturgical constraints.

The only things that are effective on the stage are those, which the spectator immediately understands. (Dürrenmatt 1998, VI, 35-36)

One hears a comedy character speak about his comedy world, but one feels inevitably reminded of all the all too real statements of top bankers and financial politicians who tried to explain to a broader public what had happened in the fall of 2008. One thinks of the numerous appeals to accept the fact that rescuing the global economy would involve measures that stand in sharp contradiction to all natural conceptions of justice. For the general public, so goes the real existing *ad spectatores* of central banks and ministries of finance in times of crisis, this all much too complicated.

And in a certain sense, this is even true. Who understands the language of, for example, the annual reports of the World Bank, for whose demonstrable tendency to become more and more unspecific Franco Moretti and Dominique Pestre have recently coined the Orwellian term *bankspeak*? (Moretti, Pestre 2015) Who would have the necessary mathematical knowledge in order to satisfactorily criticize the economic models that so obviously failed to predict the 2008 crisis? Who is able (and who is willing) to understand the reasons why the so-called system-relevant banks began to hand out absurdly huge staff bonuses, just months after their state bailout?

As a matter fact, the distinctive feature of a financial crisis, as compared to other forms of crisis, is that the discrepancy between the number of those who are affected by it and the number of those who are able to understand its dynamics is particularly high. This can be seen exemplarily in the ambivalence of the social type of the expert (cf. Macho 2014 and Kolmar 2010). His analysis and his advice are never more necessary than in the context of a crisis. And never is it more necessary to find a common language for all that falls out of the framework of his expertise, a language that enables participation on this side of expert knowledge and beyond ideological simplification. Perhaps therein lies the main contribution of Dürrenmatt's modern theater of the world to the recent discussion of the financial crisis.

What this means becomes clearer in the direct address to the audience by senior clerk Paul Böckmann. Böckmann announces a play about the abysses of high finance, which will hardly be able to cope with this matter – for no reason other than the fact that it is a *play*. But once this problem is articulated, the spectators cannot but watch the play under this very aspect. In other words, the audience is prepared to recognize the way a literary form of representation deals with its inadequacy for the representation of given problem as the actual contribution *of* literature to the discussion of this very problem.

It is no coincidence that the task of drawing the attention of the audience to this important point is reserved to the only character who, at the cost of his life, reflects on the dramaturgical logic of gangster banking. In his "Notes on *Frank V*", Dürrenmatt emphasizes that he regards the Böckmann scene as a key to the understanding of the whole play (Dürrenmatt 1998, VI, 164-65). In saying this, he clearly and exclusively had in mind the death scene, the last encounter of Frank and Böckmann and, thus, the ultimate clash between the attitude of adherence to a hopelessly bad financial capitalist comedy on the hand, and the insight into the mendacity of the claim that there are no alternatives to it on the other. What is at stake in this scene, Dürrenmatt says, is the confrontation between "rightful" and "unrightful hope" (ibid., 164).

This statement gains in importance if one considers the fact that there are *two* Böckmann scenes in this play. The first one, the direct address to the audience, is about the difficulty of representing morally problematic business practices of banks and their consequences in a generally understandable way. The second, the death scene, is about the violently tabooed insight that these practices are only seemingly without an alternative. There is obvious reason to believe that both scenes are inherently connected. The guilt that Böckmann takes upon himself has an ethical *and* a dramaturgical dimension. It consists in adhering to the false necessity of that terribly bad comedy of a private bank. In this regard, Dürrenmatt's dramaturgy of the financial crisis, in its most advanced form, advocates the rightfulness of the hope that there are (or will be) ways of dealing with the intricate connection of guilt and debt that transcend the framework of the ever-same comedy of financial capitalism.

References

Cuonz, Daniel (2018): *Die Sprache des verschuldeten Menschen. Literarische Umgangsformen mit Schulden, Schuld und Schuldigkeit.* Paderborn: Wilhelm Fink.

Der Spiegel, Hamburg, No. 32/2001.

Dupuy, Jean-Pierre (2004): *Pour un catastrophisme éclairé. Quand l'impossible est certain*. Paris: Seuil.

Dürrenmatt, Friedrich (2006): *Selected Writings*. 3 vols. Trans. Joel Agee. Chicago, IL: University of Chicago Press.

Dürrenmatt, Friedrich (1998): *Werkausgabe*. 37 vols. Zurich: Diogenes.

Dürrenmatt, Friedrich (1996): *Gespräche 1961-1990*. 4 vols. Ed. Heinz-Ludwig Arnold. Zurich: Diogenes.

Frisch, Max (1980): Romulus der Große. In: Keel, Daniel (ed.): Über Friedrich Dürrenmatt. Zurich: Diogenes, 145-47.

Horn, Eva (2014): *Zukunft als Katastrophe. Fiktion und Prävention*. Frankfurt (Main): Fischer.

Kahn, Hermann (1962): *Thinking about the Unthinkable*. New York: Horizon Press.

Kolmar, Martin (2010): Die Tragödie des glaubwürdigen Experten. *Neue Zürcher Zeitung*, 7 July 2010.

Macho, Thomas (2014): Bonds: Fesseln der Zeit. In: Macho, Thomas (ed.): *Bonds. Schuld, Schulden und andere Verbindlichkeiten*. Paderborn: Wilhelm Fink, 11-26.

Moretti, Franco, Pestre, Dominique (2015): Bankspeak. The Language of World Bank Reports. *New Left Review* 92, 75-99.

Rüedi, Peter (2011): *Dürrenmatt oder die Ahnung vom Ganzen*. Zurich: Diogenes.

Sloterdijk, Peter (2010): How Big is 'Big'? Collegium International. http://www.collegium-international.org/fr/contributions/127-how-big-is-big.html

Weber, Ulrich (2003): Dürrenmatts Endspiele. In: Centre Dürrenmatt Neuchâtel (ed.): *Dürrenmatts Endspiele. Mit Texten und Bildern von Friedrich Dürrenmatt und Beiträgen von Pierre Bühler und Ulrich Weber* Bern, 11-38.

The Order of the Derivative

Representing and Being Represented by Financialization's Sociality[1]

Max Haiven

In my inquiries into the relationship between art and money I have argued that one of the key conundrums for artists seeking to represent today's global financialized capitalist economy is that financialization itself is a process of representation (Haiven 2015a, b; Haiven 2018). Finance, as a dimension of capitalist accumulation, ultimately exists within that system to scan, interpret and respond to the vast complexity of sociality, which is to say the sublimely vast array of relationships, subjects, processes and transactions that at some point intersect "the economy". For this reason, David Harvey has analogized finance as capital's "central nervous system" (Harvey 2006). I have suggested that, perhaps, the metaphor of the imagination is more apt, in part because that term has connotations of the capacity to produce predictive images (as finance indeed does), in part because it hints at the chaos and fallibility of this image-making, in part because it also alerts us to the way financialization transforms the imagination of social actors and also relies on that transformation (Haiven 2011).

In any case, approaching "finance" as, in part, a method by which capitalism represents the social world, the better to (dis)organize it, allows us to more clearly frame the challenges facing artists who seek to represent finance or financialization. These phenomena and processes are not only mind-bogglingly baroque in their internal workings, they are also in a funny way capitalism's own inhuman form of art, or, in Bifo Berardi's

1 | This text has also been published in: Haiven, Max (2018): *Art After Money, Money After Art. Creative Strategies Against Financialization*. London: Pluto Press.

terms, poetry (Berardi 2012b). As I have argued, from one angle we can see financialization is an orchestration of the social imagination (Haiven 2014). Thus the artists who have most interested me have been those who do not seek simply to represent finance or financialization itself, but seek to investigate the relationship between finance and society, or more accurately financialization (the process by which society is recalibrated and recoded by the speculative, extractive and accelerative logics of finance) and sociality (the living, imaginative fabric of social intercourse).

With that in mind, I want here to pair the work of the radical filmmaker Melanie Gilligan and that of the late cultural theorist of financialization Randy Martin. Gilligan's 2015 film *Popular Unrest* presents a (horrifically plausible) dystopian vision of a financialized society where a vast algorithmically empowered, pre-emptive economic system (artistically personified as a singular World Spirit) colonizes not only social and economic institutions, but also the fabric of social life itself. In my reading, this film resonates strongly with Martin's theory of "derivative sociality", the forms of relationality and imagination that emerge within and are components of financialization.

Popular Unrest

Melanie Gilligan's phenomenal film *Popular Unrest* takes place in a near-future version of our society stitched together by the World Spirit, a kind of global computer system, part social network, part artificial intelligence, part temp employment agency, part global biopolitical disciplinary apparatus. Within this world, two inexplicable phenomena are occurring. First, groups of otherwise unrelated individuals from diverse walks of life start seemingly randomly gathering together based on an inexplicable but undeniable feeling of intense geniality. Second, a series of brutal knife murders are occurring, also seemingly at random, as if the killer dropped on their victims from above.

The film follows the story of one "grouping" in London as they grapple with living collectively in a world of impossible individual risk-management. In the course of the film's five episodes the true nature of the World Spirit is revealed as, essentially, the evolution of capitalism on at least three fronts. First, capitalism has encroached into the realm of the digital, collecting, collating and acting on data from an almost infinite number of inputs. In this regard the World Spirit system is capable of parsing the most minute information traces and enacting surgically precise financial and disciplinary interventions into the lifeworld it obsessively reads and catalogues. Second, the World Spirit represents capitalism in a biopolitical register, one obsessed with endless measurements of human behaviour and biometrics. The film opens with a (doomed) call-centre worker addressing an irate client frustrated about some minor penalty incurred for failing to adequately perform his economically productive health or wellbeing.

The film itself, which alternates between faux-documentary narrative and dramatic cinema, is interspliced with both news reports about current events and erratic commercials for various aspects of the World Spirit's consumer empire, most of them exhorting consumers towards financialized biopolitical imperatives such as fitness, insurance or self-improvement. Thus, the final aspect of the World Spirit is its financial dimension. "It's like money, but more money than money," explains one of the World Spirit's developers. As the film evolves we realize that the Spirit is a vast machine for crunching data and controlling bodies, all orchestrated around applying the universal measurement and solvent of a kind of money it itself has replaced as the glue that holds society together.

And yet what sort of society is it, this interconnected financialized network? The World Spirit is, of course, a sly reference to Hegel (and therefore, in a film about capitalism, to Marx), who famously theorized it as a force of modern historical consciousness acting through the aggregate sum of actions of people and forces in struggle. For Marx, of course, the World Spirit became the force of history that would bring about capitalism's downfall from within, encouraging that system to create its own gravediggers in the form of the proletariat and accelerating its own internal contradictions thanks to the chaotic motive power of inter-capitalist rivalry and bourgeois competition (Cleaver 2000). For neoliberal Hegelian Francis Fukuyama, the World Spirit was essentially synonymous with the triumphant world market which would allegedly sublimate all rivalry, conflict and tension into economic competition, resulting in ever-greater efficiency, innovation and wealth (Fukuyama 1992).

In Gilligan's portrayal, Fukuyama's dream of market freedom has become a totalitarian nightmare where the market not only reaches expansively across the globe but also intensely into daily life at the most molecular biopolitical level. Yet unlike totalitarianisms of old, formal private freedom is maintained: indeed, the World Spirit depends on and promises to facilitate the freedom of individuals to compete, to work and to self-actualize (see Haiven 2014). The economy here has fully consumed and subsumed society, aided by the ubiquitous digital surveillance and measurement technologies it, itself, has fostered. And here, the market or the economy evolves into something else entirely. With no externality, no outside, no lifeworld left to colonize, is it still the economy as we thought we knew it? When centralized in a computer system that is composed of, that measures, that can intervene in everything, is it still capitalism or that strange hybrid communized capitalism: the worst of both worlds, totalitarian closure within ruthless market insouciance? Here, the World Spirit, an allegory for financialization in my reading, both surrounds everything and is inside everything, encrypting sociality itself, transforming everything into code in order to be more advantageously orchestrated.

So ultimately the figure of the World Spirit is, in Gilligan's dystopian film, a kind of crystallized projection of tendencies immanent within our own moment of financialization. It is a projected moment when digital, biopolitical, economic and social techniques of a society of control meet and coalesce into a kind of absolute but distributed institution. For reasons of narrative, Gilligan gives a hypothetical unity to tendencies that today are more diffuse, distributed, competitive, but nonetheless just as powerful.

But, of course, something goes wrong. The World Spirit's "machine learning" algorithms are so desperate to predict, measure and leverage the minutiae of human feeling and sociality which it creates within itself that what we learn, in the course of the film, is a glitch. In Marxian terms, the inherent logic of the system produces a contradiction that manifests itself as a crisis. As with all such crises, it has dimensions of destruction (the killings) and creation (the groupings).

The Order of The Derivative

Here, Randy Martin's theorization of the social logic of the derivative is invaluable (Martin 2015a). Martin follows theorists including Dick Bryan and Michael Rafferty in posing a fundamental break in the architecture and logic of capitalism with the rise of financialization and especially with the ascendency of financialization's key technology, the derivative (Bryan/Rafferty 2006). To recap, a derivative is essentially a contract between two parties to buy or sell some asset at some future point. Conventionally and ideally, such contracts are used as a kind of insurance. For instance, a bakery might pay a fee to buy a futures contract to buy a quantity of grain at an agreed price in a year's time, therefore hedging the risk of a catastrophic increase in the price of grain. Martin perceptively points out that the derivative essentially functions to transform the future into a present-day commodity (Martin 2007). Or more accurately, the derivative allows investors to commodify and put into play multiple potential future outcomes, transforming the inherent uncertainty of entropic life into a field of quantifiable monetized risks to be managed, manipulated and, vitally, pre-empted. This pre-emptive impulse generates a new conjugation of power that creates its own field of action (see also Massumi 2015).

While derivatives have existed for millennia, under financialization they move from the periphery to the centre of the economic order. New technological and mathematical instruments have emerged that allow derivatives to be priced and exchanged as their own financial assets (MacKenzie 2006). Derivatives can be built atop one another in a portfolio, creating a complex cascade of mutually reinforcing or cantilevered speculations (Ascher 2016). They can be aggregated into complex synthetic derivatives or sliced and diced into new cuts of financial meat to suit the taste of a variety of clients. These anticipatory promissory notes, these mercenary conjectures of power, become the bedrock of a new financial system that is increasingly distant from providing the insurance and security for our hypothetical baker and that is more concerned with a constant effort towards securitization, a felicitous financial term that means the splitting apart and rebundling of assets to create new securities – as when banks disaggregated and reaggregated subprime and other loans into the infamous "mortgage-backed securities" (MBSs) they sold on to their clients as risk-free investments (see Bryan/Rafferty 2009; Haiven 2013; Martin 2007).

The example of subprime MBSs is apt because it reveals one of Martin's key points: it is not fruitful to imagine that derivatives are simply the plaything of the financialized imaginations of Wall Street or the City of London: they both reach deeply into and depend on the integration of social reality – like urban housing – into the financial fabric. Once again, here we find an example of financialization encrypting and decrypting social life, transforming the nuanced realities of poverty, policy, power, the built environment, the fabric of community, the motivation of individual borrowers and the intangible fields of hope and fear into a set of codes to be manipulated, disaggregated, reaggregated and put into play against one another. Here financialization is, as Deleuze predicted in his warnings of a Society of Control, both the "spirit of gas" that claustrophobically surrounds each and every choice in the whole process (of the politicians, of the banks, of the speculators, of the borrowers, of the regulators, of the ratings agencies), and that is also inside of them (Deleuze 1995).

For this reason, along with Bryan and Rafferty, Martin is keen to show how today derivatives essentially function as money (in the sense that they have monetary value and can command labour power) and also have tremendous impacts on the so-called "real economy" such that any artificial distinction is moot (Bryan/Rafferty 2016). Indeed, as Bryan and Rafferty show, "capitalism with derivatives" introduces new methodologies and intensifies capitalism's capacity to extract labour from workers, but does so in ways that operate under a very different logic of value than classical Marxist notions of the labour theory of value (Martin et al. 2008). For instance, the capacity of derivatives to discipline actors as diverse as small firms, large corporations and whole nation-states with speed and violence is unprecedented (LiPuma/Lee 2004; Norfield 2012). Here, value comes from the intensity of financial networks, from the ability to proliferate and interlace derivatives in ways that are socially and economically consequential, but also not directly tethered to the productive capacity or the extraction of surplus value, though this, obviously, does not mean the end of capitalist exploitation: indeed, it means its acceleration, expansion and intensification (see Lazzarato 2012; Marazzi 2010; Sassen 2014).

Leveraged Decolonization

Martin concurs, but also suggests that the ascendency of the derivative and of the shift towards financialization, of which it is the signature, is also a wholesale transformation of society and sociality itself. On the surface level, this is experienced and observed as symptomatic of the postmodern character of late capitalism: social fragmentation, hyper-alienation, the unmooring of people from place, the fluidity of identity, the precariousness of employment and life, and the becoming-asset of nearly everything (Jameson 1997, McClanahan 2016). Underneath this, Martin argues, is a completely different logic of how society and subjects are woven together. In an earlier moment of capitalism, one that Martin associates with the post-war world order, that system mobilized interlocking institutions, bureaucracies, experts and regimes of knowledge to order economic life.

This model is similar to what Deleuze identifies as Foucault's Society of Discipline (Deleuze 1995). Yet Martin notes that, by the late 1960s, manifold revolts had erupted to reject this order, which Martin, drawing on Katsiaficas, heralds as movements for decolonization (Martin 2015b). In the Global South, decolonization implied the demand for self-rule through national liberation and a rejection of formal colonial subjugation. In the Global North, these movements for decolonization took the form of struggles to refuse the conservative and exploitative conditions of social life under capitalism and state socialism, including rebellions to demand workers' autonomy, women's liberation, sexual freedom and an end to the internal colonialisms of racism. For Martin, these struggles for decolonization were characterized by demands to move together, to define new zones of autonomous sociality among the oppressed and exploited. And these movements, in sum, posed a grave existential threat to the world system as such (Berardi 2012a).

As a result, these movements became the subject of often violent repression. But, ultimately, what allowed capitalism to survive was financialization and the rise of the derivative, which reorganized the system fundamentally away from a reliance on rigid institutions and structures and towards flexible networks of control, such as Deleuze theorizes: debt is a fine example (Lazzarato 2012). On the one hand, following formal decolonization, institutions such as the International Monetary Fund and World Bank, at the behest of wealthy, former colonial nation-states, helped facilitate the "neocolonization" of the Global South through the politics of international loans, many of them odious, that essentially reinscribed Southern nations in familiar relations of extraction and control relative to the North (Bello 2013; Ndikumana/Boyce 2011). Meanwhile, in the North itself, what Boltanski and Chiapello call the "new spirit of capitalism" emerged, which promised cultural freedom of expression and individual identity within a reformed, flexible, agile capitalism which encouraged individuals to use capitalist techniques to claim freedom, creativity and autonomy through marketized means (Boltanski/Chiapello 2005). As Maurizio Lazzarato notes, this transition towards "cognitive capitalism" fundamentally relied on creating debtor subjects who "empowered" themselves in an increasingly austere, neoliberal and financialized climate by borrowing (literally and metaphorically) to invest in their human capital in the name of competition (Lazzarato 2012, see also De Angelis/Harvie 2009; Vercellone 2007).

Ultimately, then, Martin suggests that financalization emerges as a capitalist mutation to incorporate, enclose and encrypt struggle by reorganizing the economy into a decentralized, distributed, networked form based less on domineering institutions and stable (if coercive) relationships and more on fluctuating, temporary constellations of power. Finance has not only facilitated the rise of the megalithic transnational corporation, global assembly lines, disciplinary international bond markets and the ever-present threat of capital flight from those jurisdictions deemed to be insufficiently market-friendly, it has also facilitated the encroachment of monetary discipline into seemingly every aspect of social life.

For Martin, the derivative is central, not only because it enabled financialization to advance and answer the challenges of decolonization but also because it reordered social and economic life in the process. In contrast to the post-war Bretton Woods order, where large institutions (governments, corporations, state agencies, etc.) managed the lives of aggregated populations, today those populations are disaggregated and the individuals therein cross-cut by affinities, attributes and tendencies only some of which they are aware. Under an order of financialization where all our capacities and qualities are interlaced into the system through datamining, consuming practices, digital profiling, risk metrics and more, inscrutable algorithms and protocols aggregate us into communities of shared risk without our consent and often without our knowledge (O'Neil 2016; Pasquale 2015). The subprime borrowers in dozens of cities, based on a set of criteria opaque to themselves, were enrolled in a kind of silent, encrypted community that had consequences for their lives and also for the global economy.

Financialization, under the sign of the derivative, orders and organizes people and also different aspects of many people into new, cryptic aggregations all the time, constantly combining and recombining them. Metaphors for such a system are inherently inadequate, but the idea comes to mind that we are each a deck of cards, with each quality or capacity or affinity represented by one card. Financialization means the shuffling of all these cards into a huge pile while various digitally-augmented parties sort us and resort us into different piles: all the kings here, all the hearts there, all the black prime number cards here; now all the red sixes that have not been placed next to the king of clubs in four of the last seven draws; now all nines of clubs that show miniscule wear on the top left corner that are also more than 92% likely to be sandwiched between two jacks.

The logic of the derivative is one that seeks to identify, isolate and leverage these small differences, these deviances into large payback, or advantageous temporary configurations, to recognize a fragment of a pattern that can become a transformative moment. Yet – and this is crucial – the system the derivative aims to read and act upon, in this case the massive pile of cards, is the world the derivative itself has created. In other words, the derivative does not read and act upon the "real world", it creates the reality it in turn reads and acts upon. It poses itself as the means to understand and gain agency within the chaos it, itself, creates (Ayache 2010; Malik 2014). This financialized chaos, where everything *could have already been* transformed into a speculative asset to be aggregated and disaggregated, is the new order of sociality. The derivative is both its means and end: it is a methodology of sorting and leveraging that creates the effects and the sociality that, recursively, are its target.

Martin is so keen to do away with a nostalgic pining for the "old economy" of post-war Keynesianism not simply because of its manifold crimes and cruelties. He is interested in finding what potentials the sociality of the derivative might offer, what new collectivities, forms of power and social relations might emerge in the imagination and in a reality no longer tethered to dominant institutions. A pedestrian example might be the kinds of transgressive online communities that define some dimensions of their participants' belonging, identity or agency outside the conventional frameworks of nation-state, social class or even ethnicity or religion. But Martin also has something deeper and more profound in mind. He turns to the world of creative movement to discover how, in the era of financialization where the social lies in ruins, practices including modern dance, skateboarding and breakdancing emerge to explore what he calls a new "social kinaesthetics". All these forms of creative movement, he argues, cohere around a community of common risk-taking, in which participants encourage (or goad) one another to extremes precisely to discover the amorphous borders of their own potential collectivity. Modern dancers sorted by financial capitalism into gentrifying lofts, bored teenagers alienated in the suburbs slapping wheels on boards and doing stunts in abandoned backyard swimming pools, kids in the decrepit urban ghettos throwing their bodies on the pavement: all are seeking to derive some new meaning, joy, sociality and sense of common becoming from the way financialized capitalism has aggregated them together.

Securitization in Numbers

This would appear to be precisely the meaning of the groupings in Gilligan's *Popular Unrest,* and also of the killings. As the episodes unfold, it is revealed that they are the result not so much of a glitch in the World Spirit but of its own recursive efforts to learn more and parse more deeply the social fabric it, itself, is creating (which is also the economy, which is also that of the datastorm, which is also the terrain of the biopolitical). In order to better understand the murky world of human emotion and sociality, the World Spirit has created a supposed glitch within itself that aggregates people together based on arbitrary definitions such as all having made the same Amazon order on the same day (probably something even more arcane). The Killings are the by-product of this manoeuvre: as the World Spirit seeks to submit even the realm of human somatics to its scrutiny and leveraging, it loses any and all humane vestiges that may have been programmed into it, becoming fully autonomous from those who designed it. It simply executes those bodies deemed no longer useful based on its own inscrutable but terrifyingly rational derivative calculations.

All this is discovered by the grouping that the film tracks as they find themselves working with a set of scientists who claim to be trying to discover what is causing the World Spirit, which they see as a benevolent force or harmony and commerce, to glitch. In actuality, they are the agents of the Spirit's research, putting the grouping through a battery of psychologically and somatically agonizing tests to allow the Spirit to observe their individual and collective emotional reactions. In the film itself, this is represented in the form of highly fragmentary postmodern dance, where members of the group, together and individually, repeat minute gestures, reactions and forms of somatic response. Here, Gilligan's work affirms and fortifies Martin's notion of a social kinaesthetics, wherein the logic of sociality exists at the seam of individual and collective movement, at precisely the space of affects (in the Deleuzian sense of the term: the power to affect and to be affected).

Yet these experiments, and the grouping's own independent research, leads them to realize the true horrific nature of the system of which they are constituent elements: their majestic affinity emerges from the same "logic" as the murders. In the final episode, the grouping is encouraged by the scientists to "enter" into the World Spirit – which of course they were always already in – to try and tame its cruelties. This "entering" is less of a shift in geographic space and more of a kind of collective ritual. Once "inside" they learn that many other groupings have tried this before them, and that they will share their fate: repeating the mantra "I'm sorry, but I have to do this", the members of the grouping betray one another and become internalized in the World Spirit: their knowledge and experience and identity fold into its operations.

This tragic conclusion is one fate that might await us under the social logic of the derivative. It is a logic that is calibrated precisely to integrate an almost infinite diversity of actors, tendencies and ambitions. The logic of the derivative thrives not only when we commodify our dreams, energies and desires, as has happened to so many rebellious cultures, collectives and movements that have traded radicalism for participation in capitalism. The logic of the derivative thrives when it becomes the vernacular of the imagination, when its logic shapes our behaviours and decisions to make them commensurate (see Haiven 2014). A fine example here is the way that financialization leverages and weaponizes the explicitly and avowedly anti-capitalist or at least anti-consumerist ethos of independent artists and culture workers in what Stevphen Shukaitis (2015), drawing on and developing Italian autonomist theory, calls the "metropolitan factory". In a financialized context of urban property speculation, these would-be renegades become the unwitting "shock troops" of a gentrification that will, inevitably, dispose of them. The logic of the derivative is one that can fold all forms of value into its own order and logic.

The derivative, then, appears as a technique by which society – or more accurately the granular micro-practices of sociality itself – becomes increasingly encrypted. This is not, as we have observed, only a dystopian imposition from the outside but, fundamentally, relies on the self-financialization of subjects and institutions, the incorporation and application of the derivative logic from within.

Hence even the noble ambitions of the grouping, oriented as they are to reforming the World Spirit, are conscripted to its reproduction. It is notable that when one member of the grouping suggests that the World Spirit must be destroyed, a scientist scoffs: it's impossible – we *are* the World Spirit, it can't be destroyed. In the film's tragic epilogue, we learn that the grouping's revelation of the World Spirit's inherent violence has not resulted in it being shut down, but in a new global order where those people and populations that can afford to do so undertake to securitize themselves against the violence of the system of which they are a part. The rest of the world's population are left subject to the violent predation of the World Spirit (of which they are also a part). The film ends with the ominous rumours of riots and popular unrest as those who are fated to derive the system's abuses and traumas begin to rebel, and as the would-be beneficiaries beef up their securitization efforts, fighting a war on two fronts: to insulate themselves from the World Spirit, and at the same time from those who cannot insulate themselves.

Conclusion

Gilligan's vision is a dark one, but with important lessons for our current moment. Today, the mainstream political spectrum is increasingly dominated by the false alternatives of securitization. On the one hand, we are offered an acceleration of society's submission to finance, though now with none of the euphoria of the End of History or the myth of rising tides lifting all boats, simply with the candid admission that inequality will grow and grow, and that we will each be responsible for defending ourselves as best we can from the market. On the other hand, neoreactionary movements promise to wield the nation-state to defend their chosen populations from the chaos of financialization, not, of course, by creating durable models of cooperative security (such as health care, education or housing), but instead by targeting and subjugating convenient Others (migrants, racialized people, intellectuals, feminists, queer folk). As Martin observes, under financialization the historic dialectic of haves and have-nots is conjugated as the lauded risk-takers and the abject at-risk, the morbidity of the latter seen as a threat to or a drain on the vitality of the former (see also Beck 2009). Neoreactionaries ultimately respond to financialization by promising to protect and weaponize communities of risk organized around mythological and nostalgic constructs of race, nation and religion, also offering violent methods to express and diffuse the tensions and fear inherent in a derivative life of risk. They offer the promise of exclusionary collective protection from financialization. This siren song is compelling to the vast majority of people who, long ago, learned that the false cosmopolitanism of liberal financialization offers no hope. It is better to find some safety in vengeful numbers.

What is at stake now is the possibility of developing a new vision beyond the two faces of financialization as it enters terminal velocity (ecologically, socially and politically): the neoliberal, false-cosmopolitan face and the neoreactionary face. Gilligan's film offers no such vision. Martin's work offers us only the promise of new lines of solidarity and becoming that are created as a side-effect of the recoding or re-encryption of society by the derivative.

References

Ascher, Ivan (2016): *Portfolio Society. On the Capitalist Mode of Prediction.* New York: Zone Books.

Ayache, Elie (2010): *The Blank Swan. The End of Probability.* New York: Wiley.

Beck, Ulrich (2009): *World at Risk.* Cambridge/Malden, MA: Polity.

Bello, Walden (2013): *Capitalism's Last Stand? Deglobalization in the Age of Austerity.* London: Zed Books.

Berardi, Franco "Bifo" (2012a): Emancipation of the Sign. Poetry and Finance During the Twentieth Century. *E-Flux* 39, https://www.e-flux.com/journal/39/60284/emancipation-of-the-sign-poetry-and-finance-during-the-twentieth-century/.

Berardi, Franco "Bifo" (2012b): *The Uprising. On Poetry and Finance.* Los Angeles, CA: Semiotext(e).

Boltanski, Luc/Chiapello, Eve (2005): *The New Spirit of Capitalism.* Trans. Gregory Elliot. London/New York: Verso.

Bryan, Dick/Rafferty, Michael (2006): *Capitalism with Derivatives. A Political Economy of Financial Derivatives, Capital and Class.* London: Palgrave.

Bryan, Dick/Rafferty, Michael (2009): Homemade Financial Crisis. *Ephemera* 9, no. 4, 357-62.

Bryan, Dick/Rafferty, Michael (2016): Decomposing Money: Ontological Options and Spreads. *Journal of Cultural Economy* 9, no. 1, 27-42.

Cleaver, Harry (2000): *Reading Capital Politically.* Edinburgh/San Francisco, CA: AK Press.

Deleuze, Gilles (1995): Postscript to Societies of Control. In: *Negotiations,* trans. Martin Joughin. New York: Columbia University Press, 177-82.

De Angelis, Massimo/Harvie, David (2009): 'Cognitive Capitalism' and the Rat-Race. How Capital Measures Immaterial Labour in British Universities. *Historical Materialism* 17, no. 3, 3-30.

Fukuyama, Francis (1992): *The End of History and the Last Man*. New York: The Free Press.

Haiven, Max (2011): Finance as Capital's Imagination? Reimagining Value and Culture in an Age of Fictitious Capital and Crisis. *Social Text* 108, 93-124.

Haiven, Max (2013): Walmart, Finance, and the Cultural Politics of Securitization. *Cultural Politics* 9, no. 2, 239-62.

Haiven, Max (2014): *Cultures of Financialization. Fictitious Capital in Popular Culture and Everyday Life*. London/New York: Palgrave Macmillan.

Haiven, Max (2015a): Art and Money. Three Aesthetic Strategies in an Age of Financialisation. *Finance and Society* 1, no. 1, 38-60.

Haiven, Max (2015b): Money as a Medium of the Imagination. Art and the Currencies of Cooperation. In: Lovink, Geert/Tkacz, Nathaniel/De Vries, Patricia (eds.): *Moneylab Reader. An Intervention in Digital Economy*. Amsterdam: Institute of Network Cultures. http://networkcultures.org/blog/publication/moneylab-reader-an-intervention-in-digital-economy/

Haiven, Max (2018): The Crypt of Art, the Decryption of Money, the Encrypted Common and the Problem of Cryptocurrencies. In: Gloerich, Inte/Lovink, Geert/De Vries, Patricia (eds.): *Moneylab Reader 2*. Amsterdam: Institute of Network Cultures, 121-37.

Harvey, David (2006): *The Limits to Capital*. London/New York: Verso.

Jameson, Fredric (1997): Culture and Finance Capital. *Critical Inquiry* 24, no. 1, 246-65.

Lazzarato, Maurizio (2012): *The Making of the Indebted Man*. Boston, MA: MIT Press.

LiPuma, Edward/Benjamin Lee, Benjamin (2004): *Financial Derivatives and the Globalization of Risk*. Durham, NC/London: Duke University Press..

MacKenzie, Donald (2006): *An Engine, Not a Camera. How Financial Models Shape Markets*. Cambridge, MA: MIT Press.

McClanahan, Annie (2016): Dead Pledges: *Debt, Crisis, and Twenty-First-Century Culture*. Stanford, CA/London: Stanford University Press.

Malik, Suhail (2014): The Ontology of Finance: Price, Power, and the Arkhéderivative. In: Mackay, Robin (ed.): *Collapse. Vol. VIII: Casino Real.* Falmouth: Urbanomic, 629-811.

Marazzi, Christian (2010): *The Violence of Financial Capitalism.* Trans. Kristina Lebedeva. Los Angeles, CA: Semiotext(e).

Martin, Randy (2007): *An Empire of Indifference: American War and the Financial Logic of Risk Management.* Durham, NC/London: Duke University Press.

Martin, Randy (2015a): *Knowledge LTD. Towards a Social Logic of the Derivative.* Philadelphia, PA: Temple University Press.

Martin, Randy (2015b): Money after Decolonization. *South Atlantic Quarterly* 114, no. 2, 377-93.

Martin, Randy/Rafferty, Michael/Bryan, Dick (2008): Financialization, Risk and Labour. *Competition and Change* 12, no. 2, 120-32.

Massumi, Brian (2015): *Ontopower. War, Power and the States of Perception.* Durham, NC/London: Duke University Press.

Ndikumana, Léonce/Boyce, James K. (2011): *Africa's Odious Debts. How Foreign Loans and Capital Flight Bled a Continent.* London: Zed Books.

Norfield, Tony (2012): Derivatives and Capitalist Markets: The Speculative Heart of Capital. *Historical Materialism* 20, no. 1, 103-32.

O'Neil, Cathy (2016): *Weapons of Math Destruction. How Big Data Increases Inequality and Threatens Democracy.* New York: Crown.

Pasquale, Frank (2015): *The Black Box Society. The Secret Algorithms That Control Money and Information.* Cambridge, MA: Harvard University Press.

Sassen, Saskia (2014): *Expulsions. Brutality and Complexity in the Global Economy.* Cambridge, MA: Harvard University Press.

Shukaitis, Stevphen (2015): Art Strikes and the Metropolitan Factory. In: Kozłowski, Michał et al. (eds.): *The Political Economy of Social Creativity.* London: MayFly Books/Ephemera, 227-36.

Vercellone, Carlo (2007): From Formal Subsumption to General Intellect. Elements for a Marxist Reading of the Thesis of Cognitive Capitalism. *Historical Materialism* 15, no. 1, 13-36.

Financial Markets as Interpretative Economies

An Overview of the Meaning of Financialized Money

Andreas Langenohl

Money, Finance and Meaning

This article discusses the question of money as a question of financial semiosis. As Aaron Sahr (2017) has recently pointed out, since the end of the Bretton Woods agreement, money has increasingly become financialized money, that is, fiat money produced by commercial banks by giving out loans within the horizon of financial investment rationalities. Talking about the meaning of money, he implies, crucially involves talking about the meaning of finance.

The paper represents an attempt to systematize social-scientific accounts and conceptualizations that revolve around the semiotic dimension of financialized money. It will therefore deal less with everyday practices of using money and lending it social and cultural significance (cf., for instance, Zelizer 1994). The main context of the paper is instead as follows. Social-scientific accounts of financial market dynamics have been revolving around the question of how to most adequately conceptualize practices of meaning-making in financial markets. Since some time now, financial economies have been understood as symbolic economies, in which the production of and trade in material commodities is replaced by the production of value symbols (prices). According to other accounts, the ways that financial markets operate emanate from 'performative' effects of economic theorizing and modelling, to the effect that markets are, in Michel Callon's famous phrase, 'embedded in economics' (Callon 1998). Still from a different perspective, financial markets have been reconstructed as particular types of publics, capitalizing on the argument that financial dynamics cannot be understood without taking into account the different audience segments, and more generally the public (re-)presentation of financial markets, that form and negotiate expectations regarding the valuation of financial products. Lastly, the financial economy has been characterized as an economy of fictions, an approach that stresses the speculative, imaginative and anticipatory logic of financial investments. Social-scientific approaches to the financial economy have thus tended to reconstruct the particularities of financial markets and their interrelation with other sectors of the economy and of society at large within a, broadly and variously understood, semiotic idiom.

After having reconstructed this context, the paper will conclude by suggesting an understanding of financial markets as an economy of the *unreal*. The term 'unreal' will be developed in an, only seemingly paradoxical, interrelation with an analysis of techniques of the empirical that characterize current practices of financial valuation. The main point will be that financial dynamics are fueled by discrepancies between empirically grounded technologies of valuation and a sense of the future as uncertain.

Financial Markets as Semiotic Economies: On 'Decoupling'

For some time now, economic sociology has attempted to wrest away the analysis of economic processes from economics, especially in its neoclassical variety. In general, the strategy used in this endeavor has been to point out that markets are, in an influential formulation by Karl Polanyi (1944), 'embedded' in larger societal structures, thus challenging the tendency of neoclassical economics to epistemologically isolate markets and reconstruct them through incremental models (Fligstein 2002; Granovetter 1985). Important contributions to this strand of sociological theorizing have been the argument that markets resemble orders of mutual observation of competitors who orient their action toward one another (White 2002a, b), and that economic actors within a given market attempt to keep potential competitors at bay (Fligstein 2001). Markets have also been typologized with respect to different forms of knowledge that inform action within them (Aspers 2007), and more generally analyzed with respect to the 'conventions' that enable economic actors to valuate commodities (cf. Diaz-Bone 2015).

In some contrast to this sociological approach, the politico-economic analysis of financial markets has formulated a perspective that foregrounds not the embeddedness of markets, but instead their decoupling from the production-based economy (cf. Strange 1986). An important example of this style of analysis has been given by Manuel Castells (1996), who, in his analysis of 'informational capitalism', diagnoses a double shift in the general economic order in historically western, capitalist societies. On the one hand, in informational capitalism the production and exchange of material commodities tends to be replaced by the production and circulation of financial instruments that have a purely symbolic ontology, so that profit is made not through the sale of commodities but through a rise in the price of those instruments (Knorr Cetina 2007). On the other hand, the expansion of the financial sector made possible by the extension of computerized and real-time communication technologies increasingly dominates the profit logic of the economy at large, so that the industrial rationality of profit maximization (optimization of the relationship between capital input and commodity output) is supplanted by the said principle of profit maximization by driving up the value of financial assets (Davis 2009). This shift in the politico-economic dynamics of capitalist economies has been taken as a point of departure for various diagnoses that term financial capitalism "casino capitalism" (Strange 1986), observe a 'desubstantialization' (*Entstofflichung*, Albert et al. 1999) of global economic dynamics, or depict the emergence of a complete parallel universe of financial capitalism cutting all ties with the production-based economy (Baudrillard 1992).

In order to align the politico-economic theorem of financial decoupling with the approach in economic sociology that insists on the embeddedness of markets, it is useful to distinguish between two perspectives on financial markets that focus on the constitution and the continuation of financial markets respectively (cf. Langenohl 2009). On the one hand, it has been shown in the social studies of finance (a field of research to which I will return below) that pricing – which can be regarded as the core mechanism of financial markets – presupposes a whole apparatus of social, political and economic institutions that cannot be reduced to the markets themselves. The related claim that "[a] price is a social thing" (Beunza/Hardie/MacKenzie 2006) refers to various socio-technological arrangements and routines that must be in place before price formation can even begin. These include, as Saskia Sassen (1991; 2005) has shown, the technological, legal, economic and communicative institutions typically to be found in global cities, such as IT networks, stock exchanges, company headquarters, legal firms, advertising companies, or even the maintenance services that look after the buildings that house financial institutions and the private service sector catering to the needs and desires of financial professionals. Furthermore, it has been argued that pricing presupposes the presence of standards of economic calculation and financial commensuration (Beunza/Hardie/MacKenzie 2006; Riles 2011) which establish comparabilities, and thus enable trading streams, between different financial products and market segments. It is thus safe to say that financial markets, regarding their *constitution*, are embedded in manifold institutions not of their own making and rationality.

At the same time, these arguments do not sufficiently explain the mode of *continuation* of financial markets, which resides in the way that price signals interlock and respond to one another. Financialized money is based on the circulation of price signals (interest rates, stock market price data, prices for derivatives and their risk components, etc.). Financial practice thus is in accordance with finance as a discipline, whose main concern is 'pricing', that is, the theorization and calculation of 'adequate' prices for financial assets, liabilities and securities. Pricing is thus the material base of the financial economy; but its dynamics cannot be fully explained by pointing to its institutional preconditions. Elsewhere (Langenohl 2009) I have argued that those dynamics can be reconstructed through an argument addressing the semiotic structure of prices, namely, as 'signals'. The notion of 'signal' here has a terminological significance, derived from George Herbert Mead's (1988) discussion of the difference between signal communication and symbol communication. A signal is a form of communication not *intended* as communication, but *perceived* to be one. Unlike symbols, which, according to Mead, must have a meaning both for the sender and for the receiver in order to engender action coordination, signals trigger reactions that cannot be linked back to the sender's motivation. This is exactly the condition of financial pricing. It is a process in which prices emerge on the basis of a mathematical calculus that interrelates supply and demand, which are then taken as frames of reference for further trading, yet in the absence of the possibility to understand, let alone question, the motives behind all those trades that result in a given price. Price signals therefore cannot be effectively questioned as they conceal the motivations and action orientations underlying the decisions whose accumulated effects formed them in the first place.

It is thus possible to argue that financial markets do effect a semiotic closure, catering to the diagnosis of their decoupling from the production-based economy, because it is through such semiotic decoupling that finance attains its particular mode of economicity, understood as the radical play of supply and demand for securities. Yet at the same time, the decoupling argument does not apply to various other links that financial markets entertain with the world around them. This applies to various facets of financial markets, to be discussed below: the performing of markets through non-market generated means (performative meaning) and the ways that they trigger professional subjectivations; the role of financial audiences authorized to interpret market signals; and ultimately the question of what kind of non-financial ontology finance needs to presuppose, and helps to engender, for its own functioning.

The Social Studies of Finance: Between Performativity and Subjectivation

Some of the most important recent contributions to the socio-scientific research on financial markets, and on their dimensions of meaning, have come from a field called the social studies of finance (SSF). In very general terms, SSF approaches argue that financial processes engage particular dimensions of sociality which enter into complex interrelations with the cognitive-technological setup of financial markets. I wish to differentiate between two major strands in SSF, which refer to, first, the reconstruction of the ways that financial markets are 'performed' within their techno-social cognitive milieu, and second, to the subject positions and identities enabled in and by that milieu. This, of necessity incomplete, characterization of SSF will help flesh out the ways in which questions of meaning-making are channeled into the study of the financial economy.

First, SSF has foregrounded the ways in which financial dynamics have been constituted by an interplay of financial modelling, developed in the sphere of academic finance, and increasingly computerized real-time trading. A major focus of attention has been prominent models of financial pricing, such as the Black-Scholes formula for option pricing developed and refined in the course of the 1970s (cf. the article by Born in this volume). MacKenzie and Millo (2003) argue that this model unfolded a 'performative' logic: the more its calculus became practically applicable through increasing computation capacity, and the more it was consequently used by traders, the more its model estimations approximated pricing realities. Some arguments regarding the necessity to create a social substrate of trade-willing individuals in order to set up financial markets notwithstanding (MacKenzie/Millo 2003), SSF broadly chooses to see the prerequisites for financial markets in such amalgams of scienticized market models and their technological inflation through larger computation capacities (cf. MacKenzie 2004). Proceeding from these findings, MacKenzie (2008) maintain that finance-related models are less theories to understand market dynamics than instruments to set them in motion. SSF thus takes up an earlier argument by Michel Callon (1998) that the economy is not theorized by, but performatively embedded in economics as a set of cognitive devices that enable numerical calculations on the basis of distinctions ('framing') of what belongs to the economy as a rationed endeavor, and what does not. Within this first strand, SSF thus puts the emphasis on socio-scientific-technological 'market devices' (Callon/Millo 2007) that enable highly technologized, and in their calculative procedures ever more automatized, financial markets.

Second, financial markets have been described to call forth, and to enable, particular ways in which financial professionals can relate to them that have a substantial potential for identification and subjectivation. In a series of studies, Knorr Cetina and Bruegger (2000, 2002a, b) have argued that traders tend to maintain an affective relationship to the markets precisely because the latter offer no indication of the motivational structure underlying their dynamics (see above). In this context, the screens that relate market movements to traders play an important role, as they render the market as an object that can never be seen in its entirety but only partially discloses itself as ever emerging (cf. also Arnoldi 2006 and Langenohl/Schmidt-Beck 2007). Markets are thus conceptualized as cognitively and affectively significant objects that not only allow, but demand, a constant re-subjectivation in a recursive loop between attempts to interpret and to 'see' the market and the latter's self-effacement. In this respect, it has also been pointed out that financial subjectivities and identities form in response to certain aspects of market processes, such as their temporal horizons, that engage financial professionals in different strategies of sequencing, anticipating and rationalizing market movements (Langenohl 2008; Langenohl/Schmidt-Beck 2007; Miyazaki

2007). Earlier on, Abolafia (1996) had argued that financial markets and their techno-social setup engender a milieu that invites traders to pursue the positionality of a 'hyper-rational' economic subjectivity. Differentiating the argument of market-related subjectivation and identification processes further, Wansleben (2013) offers an exemplary ethnographic account of how different financial professionalisms (analysts and traders) in banks' financial departments pursue different positionalities vis-à-vis the market and in collaboration with one another.

For the purposes of this article, I suggest reconstructing the SSF research agenda with respect to how it fanned out from the earlier agenda of science and technology studies (STS). Many scholars working in this field started their ethnographic careers not on trading floors but in laboratories, or took decisive inspiration from conceptual work based on research from 'laboratory life'. From this point of view, the focus on financial market-driven subjectivation processes, foregrounded by Knorr Cetina and others, appears as a continuation of earlier work on how the relationship between researchers, their instruments and the substances they scrutinize enables the taking of affective and moral positionalities (Knorr Cetina 1997). Conversely, the debate about the performativity of financial economics might be seen as resembling in some instances the earlier focus in STS on the socio-scientific production of scientific facts, as in Rheinberger's (2001) classic study on the 'discovery' of DNA or similar work by Bruno Latour (1979). Both the STS approach and the performativity theorem refuse a correspondence-theoretical model of the relation between science and (scientific or financial) facts, and instead favor a model that describes of how one affects and effects the other. The more recent debates about different types of financial performativity, or the question of the conditions under which economic theories and models effect financial processes (for instance, those of pricing) so that those processes resemble the model (MacKenzie/Muniesa/Siu 2007), distract attention from the more fundamental conviction that financial economics is part of the production process of finance, not merely its academic reflection (a point which, by all likelihood, financial economics would subscribe to, too, cf. Langenohl 2018).

SSF, in both of its strands as identified here, tends to follow the same line as STS in another respect. To a certain degree, both sidestep the wider embeddedness of finance within society and the economy at large, so emphasizes by more politico-economic accounts (see above), instead giving prevalence to the more circumscribed site of financial markets, financial economics developing in tandem with the markets, and financial professionalism. They expose the techno-social "microstructures" (Knorr Cetina/Bruegger 2002b) of the financial economy, and they do so both with respect to semiotic complementarities between financial theory, financial practice and financial professionalism as well as with a view to the frictions between those components of the financial economy; however, they only very rarely consider the broader societal and cultural effects of financial practices. Accordingly, these important accounts ought to be supplemented by approaches that look into how financial meaning-making transcends the realm of finance. This is the concern of research referred to the next section.

Financial Publics

Price signals alone do not deliver the keys to their interpretation; unlike symbol communication, they do not carry with them interpretive frames and communicative feedback loops that would help to assure the adequacy of a given frame of interpretation. In this sense, while the continuation of financial markets is based on the signal character of price communication, the latter is often insufficient to 'make sense' of prices. This pertains, at least, to public communication on financial markets, which always refers to additional registers of meaning – discourses – in order to make sense of the markets (Langenohl 2009).

Thus it would be misleading to assume that public communication in the horizon of financial markets is similar to political public communication. Instead, pricing makes audiences emerge that are fundamentally different in their composition and imaginary reach from the 'ordinary' public sphere. To be sure, many studies have reconstructed evidence that financial audiences and political audiences, at times, overlap, at least in terms of their normative claims. For instance, Peebles (2008) has argued that toward the end of the 19th century, the practice of hoarding valuables and money, through the introduction of national currencies, was actively discouraged by national governments who had an interest in pooling the nation's assets, brought about mainly through the institutionalization of savings banks. It has also been argued that financial investment has been framed as a mode of participation in a society's opportunity structures, so that the projects of economic development, financial wellbeing and societal participation could be aligned by expanding the number of private investors in securities (Aitken 2007; Langley 2015). These studies document attempts to wed the enlargement of financial audiences to the inflation of claims to collective, mostly national, morality. Yet, their accounts must be questioned under conditions of profoundly financialized money, that is, money created by commercial banks within a horizon of financial opportunity.

In this constellation, it makes sense to introduce the concept of "financial publics" or "financial audiences" (*Finanzmarktöffentlichkeiten, Finanzmarktpublika,* cf. Langenohl 2009 and Langenohl/Wetzel 2014). These publics or audiences gather around a shared point of concern and focus of attention, which is the volatile pricing dynamics of financial markets. They are generally constituted by institutional investors (for instance, asset management firms or insurance companies) and professional agencies setting interpretive frames, such as rating agencies and central banks. Under conditions of increased public attention to financial dynamics, they may also encompass economic experts, political actors or social movement organizations (cf. Graeber 2013; Grusin 2010; Maesse 2017); yet what is peculiar to them is a semiotic recursivity between public statements and pricing dynamics. Financial publics are thus not given, but emerge in a field of resonance between pricing dynamics and public communications that are attributed to be influenced by those pricing dynamics, or conversely to have an effect on them. In those audiences, price signals enter into a recursive loop with public statements, so that the price signals and statements come to be seen as reacting to and commenting on each other (Langenohl 2017).

Financial publics thus can be regarded as a major entry point for financial semiosis into a much broader array of public communication. While actors and institutions may gain authorization through being held eligible for entering into resonance with pricing dynamics, their public communications tend to be reduced to the question of how they reflect, trigger or respond to pricing dynamics. Authorization in the financial public thus operates on a valorization of price signals as 'meaningful' public communication. This tends to colonize genuinely political discourse, as the latter is seen mainly in its quality as a trigger for market movements, while the coordinates within which this triggering occurs are reproduced through the afore-mentioned recursivity (cf. Kädtler 2014). This could also be an explanation for the, so far, largely failed attempts by counter-publics to disturb the profit maximization logic of financialized capitalism – their communications were hardly held eligible for entering into resonance with pricing dynamics (cf. Pianta 2013).

Financial Fictions

Financial markets have often been reproached for operating not on economic facts, but on economic fictions. In particular, various studies have pointed out that financial products attain their economic value through forecasts. From this point of view, financial investments appear as bets on their future value; accordingly, financial markets are driven not by any 'underlying' economic value (such as, in the case of company shares or company bonds, a company's market performance in the production-based economy) but by instruments that price potential future value developments into current values (such as options, futures or swaps). These so-called financial derivatives thus appear to be the operational core of the financial economy; as they trade on potentialities that might, but also might not, become true, the whole financial economy appears to be based on "fictional expectations" regarding the future value of financial assets (Beckert 2014; Esposito 2010; Lee/LiPuma 2004).

The concept of fictivity, however, is a double-edged sword. On the one hand, it helps to understand that the financial economy is based on speculations, anticipations and imaginations; and consequently, it invites the exceedingly important question of how these anticipations and imaginations, as fictitious ones, can be stabilized and maintained even in the face of recurrent criticisms of such speculative logic (Boy 2014; de Goede 2005). On the other hand, the notion of fictivity invokes a juxtaposition that renders the financial economy somewhat 'less real' than the production-based economy. Yet it has been argued above that financial markets are a 'real' economy precisely in the sense of the materiality of pricing (cf. Beunza/Hardie/Mackenzie 2006). On a deeper level, we may even say that "informational capitalism" (Castells 1996) has its own materialism, in the sense that processes of communication form its material-social basis. If one wants to critique financial markets for their, arguably very volatile and sometimes devastating, dynamics, then this cannot be done through the juxtaposition of economy fictivity and economic reality, as that fictivity disposes of a realness in its own right. In the concluding section, I thus want to propose an alternative concept to critically come to terms with financial dynamics, and to develop it in the framework of the more general interest in meaning-making practices at financial markets. I will suggest that what distinguishes financial markets and their practices of valuation is not so much their fictivity but rather their *unrealness.*

The Empirical Reaching Out into the Unreal

Reviewing recent literature on 'disaster capitalism', Arjun Appadurai (2013) has argued that financial market valuation maintains a paradoxical relationship to techniques of producing empirical data. As 'disaster capitalism' bets on the probabilities of future catastrophes (for instance, through derivatives that are coupled to estimations and forecasts in the insurance and reinsurance sector), it deploys calculative practices (such as risk assessment) which translate catastrophic potentialities into calculable value signifiers that can then be traded on markets (cf. also Aitken 2011). The data thus produced are 'empirical' in the sense that the forecasts are based on methodologies that claim to be grounded in calculable facts. Another example of a similar logic that invokes the empirical is mathematical finance, which disassembles financial products into their risk components, creating new products through the construction of different types of risk that are conceptually differentiated from one another (for instance, risks regarding default or loss in value of a given security, cf. Langenohl 2018).

Obviously, these procedures constructing the empirical from analyses of data align with the 'fictivity' of financial valuation; they could thus be called techniques of the production of fictions. In the research literature, this has, since Keynes (1997), been viewed with suspicion, namely as a more or less deliberate denial of the general unknowability of the future, that is, its 'uncertainty' (Kessler 2010). From this point of view, financial strategies of the empirical miss out on the fundamental fact that the future cannot be known and that their forecasts are thus highly susceptible to the future's contingency. Yet I would point out that it is precisely the unknowability of the future that fuels financial dynamics. 'Disaster capitalism', for instance, bets on such unknowability, so that unknowability *per se* becomes the main semiotic means of production of financial instruments. In other words, the point is not that financial products are based on an erroneous temporal ontology, but that they are based on a full *appraisal* of the future's contingency.

Seen from this angle, the methodologies to construct the financial empirical entail an understanding that their operative value consists precisely in the *limits* they have when facing future contingency. Only under the condition that the empirical is never coterminous with future realities can it be put to work in trading those realities as an array of possibilities. The notion of 'resilience', recently often invoked in reconceptualizations of financial governance in the wake of the world financial crisis, is thus already a reflection not so much of the fictivity of expectations, but more of the necessity to anticipate the unreal, precisely as that which *cannot* and *must not* be known, on the basis of the acknowledgment of the limits of empirical knowledge. The production value of empirical financial strategies is their non-coincidence with the future real; or, as we might also say, they are productive inasmuch they refer to the *unreal*.

I therefore suggest replacing the notion of 'fiction' in the analysis of the semiotic dimension of financialized money with that of the 'unreal'. Fiction, while oscillating between imagination and lie (Boy 2014) and following its own meaning devices (narrative structures, for instance), maintains an, if indirect and often fleeting, connection to the non-fictive. Its meaning is bound to non-fiction precisely in its quality *as* fiction, generating significance from the discord between fiction and non-fiction. By way of contrast, the unreal refers to a modality of meaning that seemingly directly emanates from the twists of the 'empirical' and thrives on the latter's necessary incompleteness. The discrepancy between the empirical and the unreal is not that of a tension held in permanence between an account and that to which it refers; instead, the unreal is seen as being juxtaposed to what can be construed on 'empirical' grounds. This way, the unreal attains the significance not of a possible reality, but of a bet on *im*possibility that informs present action.

References

Abolafia, Mitchell Y. (1996): Hyper-rational Gaming. *Journal of Contemporary Ethnography* 25, 226-50.

Aitken, Rob (2011): Financializing security: Political prediction markets and the commodification of uncertainty. *Security Dialogue* 42, no. 2, 123-41.

Aitken, Rob (2007): *Performing Capital: Toward a Cultural Economy of Popular and Global Finance.* New York: Palgrave.

Albert, Mathias et al. (1999): *Die neue Weltwirtschaft: Entstofflichung und Entgrenzung der Ökonomie.* Frankfurt (Main): Suhrkamp.

Appadurai, Arjun (2013): *The Future as Cultural Fact: Essays on the Global Condition.* London/New York: Verso.

Arnoldi, Jakob (2006): Frames and Screens: the Reduction of Uncertainty in Electronic Derivatives Trading. *Economy and Society* 35, no. 3, 381-99.

Aspers, Patrik (2007): Wissen und Bewertung auf Märkten. *Berliner Journal für Soziologie* 17, 431-49.

Baudrillard, Jean (1992): *Der unmögliche Tausch.* Berlin: Merve.

Beckert, Jens (2013): Imagined futures: Fictional expectations in the economy. *Theory and Society* 42, no. 3, 219-40.

Beckert, Jens (2014): *Capitalist Dynamics: Fictional Expectations and the Openness of the Future.* MPIfG Discussion Paper 14/7. Cologne: Max-Planck-Institut für Gesellschaftsforschung.

Beunza, Daniel/Hardie, Iain/MacKenzie, Donald (2006): A Price is a Social Thing: Towards a Material Sociology of Arbitrage. *Organization Studies* 27, no. 5, 721-45.

Boy, Nina (2014): Öffentlichkeit als public credit. In: Langenohl, Andreas/ Wetzel, Dietmar J. (eds.): *Finanzmarktpublika. Moralität, Krisen und Teilhabe in der ökonomischen Moderne.* Wiesbaden: Springer VS, 301-17.

Callon, Michel (1998): An Essay on Framing and Overflowing. In: Callon, Michel (ed.): *The Laws of the Market.* Oxford/Malden, MA: Blackwell, 244-69.

Callon, Michel/Millo, Yuval (eds.) (2007): *Market Devices.* Oxford/Malden, MA: Blackwell.

Castells, Manuel (1996): *The Information Age: Economy, Society and Culture. Vol. 1.: The Rise of the Network Society.* Oxford/Malden, MA: Blackwell.

Davis, Gerald F. (2009): *Managed by the Markets: How Finance Re-Shaped America.* Oxford/New York: Oxford University Press.

De Goede, Marieke (2005): *Virtue, Fortune and Faith: A Genealogy of Finance.* Minneapolis, MN/London: University of Minnesota Press.

Diaz-Bone, Rainer (2015): *Die "Economie des conventions". Grundlagen und Entwicklungen der neuen französischen Wirtschaftssoziologie.* Wiesbaden: Springer VS.

Esposito, Elena (2010): *Die Zukunft der Futures. Die Zeit des Geldes in Finanzwelt und Gesellschaft.* Heidelberg: Carl-Auer-Systeme.

Fligstein, Neil (2001): *The Architecture of Markets: An Economic Sociology of Twenty-First-Century Capitalist Societies.* Princeton, NJ: Princeton University Press.

Fligstein, Neil (2002): Agreements, Disagreements, and Opportunities in the "New Sociology of Markets". In: Mauro F. Guillén/Randall Collins/Paula England/Marshall Meyer (eds.): *The New Economic Sociology: Developments in an Emerging Field.* New York: Russell Sage Foundation, 61-78.

Graeber, David (2013): *The Democracy Project: A History. A Crisis. A Movement.* London/New York: Penguin.

Granovetter, Mark (1985): Economic action and social structure: the problem of embeddedness. *American Journal of Sociology* 91, no. 3, 481-510.

Grusin, Richard (2010): *Premediation: Affect and Mediality After 9/11.* Basingstoke/New York: Palgrave Macmillan.

Kädtler, Jürgen (2014): Finanzmarktöffentlichkeit und Finanzmarktrationalität. Zu den Bestandsbedingungen einer Form bedingter Rationalität in der Krise. In: Langenohl, Andreas/Wetzel, Dietmar J. (eds.): *Finanzmarktpublika. Moralität, Krisen und Teilhabe in der ökonomischen Moderne.* Wiesbaden: Springer VS, 173-95.

Kessler, Oliver (2010): Risk. In: Burgess, J. Peter (ed.): *The Routledge Handbook of New Security Studies.* London/New York: Routledge, 17-16.

Keynes, John Maynard (1997 [1936]): *The General Theory of Employment, Interest, and Money.* Amherst: Prometheus.

Knorr Cetina, Karin (1997): Sociality with objects: social relations in post-social knowledge societies. *Theory, Culture & Society* 14, no. 1, 1-30.

Knorr Cetina, Karin (2007): Economic Sociology and the Sociology of the Finance, *Economic Sociology. The European Economic Newsletter* 8, no. 3, 4-10.

Knorr Cetina, Karin/Bruegger, Urs (2000): The Market as an Object of Attachment: Exploring Postsocial Relations in Financial Markets. *Canadian Journal of Sociology* 25, no. 2, 141-68.

Knorr Cetina, Karin/Bruegger, Urs (2002a): Traders' Engagement with Markets: A Postsocial Relationship. *Theory, Culture & Society* 19, no. 5/6, 161-85.

Knorr Cetina, Karin/Bruegger, Urs (2002b): Global Microstructures: The Virtual Societies of Financial Markets. *American Journal of Sociology* 107, no. 4, 905-50.

Langenohl, Andreas (2008): "In the long run we are all dead:" Imaginary time in financial market narratives. *Cultural Critique* 70, 3-31.

Langenohl, Andreas (2009): Finanzmarktöffentlichkeiten. Die funktionale Beziehung zwischen Finanzmarkt und öffentlichem Diskurs. In: Rainer Diaz-Bone/Gertraude Krell (eds.): *Diskurs und Ökonomie. Diskursanalytische Perspektiven auf Märkte und Organisationen.* Wiesbaden: Springer VS, 245-66.

Langenohl, Andreas (2017): Securities markets and political securitization: The case of the sovereign debt crisis in the Eurozone. *Security Dialogue* 48, no. 2, 131-48.

Langenohl, Andreas (2018): Sources of financial synchronism: Arbitrage theory and the promise of risk-free profit. In: Klöckner, Christian/ Müller, Stefanie (eds.): *Financial Times.* Special issue of *Finance & Society* 4, no. 1, 124-42.

Langenohl, Andreas/Schmidt-Beck, Kerstin (2007): Technology and (post-)sociality in the financial market: A re-evaluation. *Science, Technology and Innovation Studies* 3, no. 1, 5-22.

Langenohl, Andreas/Wetzel, Dietmar J. (eds.) (2014): *Finanzmarktpublika. Moralität, Krisen und Teilhabe in der ökonomischen Moderne.* Wiesbaden: Springer VS.

Langley, Paul (2015): *Liquidity Lost: The Governance of the Global Financial Crisis.* Oxford: Oxford University Press.

Latour, Bruno (1979): *Laboratory Life: The Construction of Scientific Facts.* Beverly Hills, CA: Sage.

Lee, Benjamin/LiPuma, Edward (2004): *Financial Derivatives and the Globalization of Risk.* Durham, NC/London: Duke University Press.

MacKenzie, Donald (2004): The Big, Bad Wolf and the Rational Market: Portfolio Insurance, the 1987 Crash and the Performativity of Economics. *Economy and Society* 33, no. 3, 303-34.

MacKenzie, Donald (2008): *An Engine, Not a Camera: How Financial Models Shape Markets.* Boston, MA: MIT Press.

MacKenzie, Donald/Millo, Yuval (2003): Constructing a Market, Performing Theory: The Historical Sociology of a Financial Derivatives Exchange. *American Journal of Sociology* 109, no. 1, 107-45.

MacKenzie, Donald/Muniesa, Fabian/Siu, Luca (eds.) (2007): *Do Economists Make Markets? On the Performativity of Economics,* Princeton, NJ: Princeton University Press, 311-57.

Maesse, Jens (2017): Austerity discourses in Europe: how economic experts create identity projects. *Innovation: The European Journal of Social Science Research*, 1-17.

Mead, George Herbert (1988 [1934]): *Geist, Identität und Gesellschaft*, 7th edition. Frankfurt (Main): Suhrkamp.

Miyazaki, Hirokazu (2007): Between arbitrage and speculation: an economy of belief and doubt. *Economy and Society* 36, no. 3, 396-415.

Peebles, Gustav (2008): Inverting the panopticon: Money and the nationalization of the future. *Public Culture* 20, no. 2, 233-65.

Pianta, Mario (2013): Democracy lost: The financial crisis in Europe and the role of civil society. *Journal of Civil Society* 9, no. 2, 148-61

Polanyi, Karl (1944): *The Great Transformation*. Foreword by Robert M. MacIver. New York: Farrar & Rinehart.

Rheinberger, Hans-Jörg (2001): *Experimentalsysteme und epistemische Objekte. Eine Geschichte der Proteinsynthese im Reagenzglas*. Göttingen: Wallstein Verlag.

Riles, Annelise (2011): *Collateral Knowledge: Legal Reasoning in the Global Financial Markets*. Chicago, IL/London: University of Chicago Press.

Sahr, Aaron (2017): *Das Versprechen des Geldes: Eine Praxistheorie des Kredits*. Hamburg: Hamburger Edition.

Sassen, Saskia (1991): *The Global City. New York, London, Tokyo*. Princeton, NJ: Princeton University Press.

Sassen, Saskia (2005): The Embeddedness of Electronic Markets: The Case of Global Capital Markets. In: Knorr Cetina, Karin/Preda, Alex (eds.): *The Sociology of Financial Markets*. Oxford/New York: Oxford University Press, 17-37.

Strange, Susan (1986): *Casino Capitalism*. Oxford: Blackwell.

Wansleben, L. (2013): *Cultures of Expertise in Global Currency Markets*. London/New York: Routledge.

White, Harrison C. (2002a): Markets and Firms: Notes Toward the Future of Economic Sociology. In: Guillén, Mauro F./Collins, Randall/England, Paula/Meyer, Marshall (eds.): *The New Economic Sociology: Developments in an Emerging Field*. New York: Russell Sage Foundation, 129-47.

White, Harrison C. (2002b): *Markets from Networks: Socioeconomic Models of Production*. Princeton, NJ/Oxford: Princeton University Press.

Zelizer, Viviana A. (1994): *The Social Meaning of Money: Pin Money, Paychecks, Poor Relief, & Other Currencies*. New York: Basic Books.

Trades

Interview with Imanuel Schipper (Hamburg)

Jörg Metelmann:
The questions in this volume deal with how money, or economics, can be visualized. That's also one of the main issues you and *Rimini Protokoll* focus on. Do you remember the first time the problem was consciously addressed during your discussions or in your work?

Imanuel Schipper:
My first encounter with *Rimini Protokoll* was in 2002, when I co-produced *Shooting Bourbaki*, a play about *Knabenschiessen* [a traditional target shooting competition] in Zurich. During this event, the organizers try to get young boys excited about shooting military-grade guns offering prizes they couldn't afford otherwise. Prizes, promises, and trade are elementary features of every theater dramaturgy, not just at *Rimini Protokoll*. But the economy always had a special significance, especially in hindsight. The question of how much funerals cost arose early on, during the following production, *Deadline* (2003), a play about the average western European death. In it, the mayor starts talking about how a crematorium could save his city from going broke. And in *Sonde Hannover* (2002), a play about an observation station above the main shopping district in Hanover, an economist discusses how expensive shopping is, why we keep buying more and more things, and to what extent a shoplifter creates jobs for store security. A few years later, we discussed *Wallenstein* (2005) and how expensive wars are. During the Thirty Years' War, a siege took as long as you could feed your soldiers: if you had money, you could add another week of sieging. During that time, a coin's symbolic value became separate from its physical value (silver, for example). Ever since that production, economics has played a role again and again. At some point we wondered if, to what extent and how money could be an interesting topic for the stage. This

thought led us to take a closer look at Marx's *Capital*, and to the production *Karl Marx: Das Kapital, Erster Band* (2006). And the preparations for that production led to a visit to a Deutsche Bank general meeting, where the idea for producing *Hauptversammlung* (2009) emerged.

Jörg Metelmann:
What tools, which theatrical devices, did you use to answer that question?

Imanuel Schipper:
The preparation process is more similar to research in journalism, rather than academic research where you consult literature. We often deal with complex phenomena that we don't know and don't understand. That's why we reach out to different experts for advice and explanations; to people who know much more than we do. A lot of the time, getting them to lend us an hour of their time, that's the biggest challenge. In the lives of experts, time has a bigger economic value, as opposed to money.

Capital was about what money actually is, and we tried to figure that out, asking a few experts. Again and again, we were met with surprise and a lack of understanding: Why would anybody want to bring something to the stage that's so dry? But after *Wallenstein*, Schiller's three-volume opus magnum, we were looking for a new challenge. I think I'd call "being overwhelmed" a leitmotif when working with *Rimini Protokoll*. When we decided on *Capital*, we knew that none of us had read the book and probably never would read the entire text. I listened to a reading of it when I went running one time. With this utter zero-knowledge, we met with several experts and asked them what they thought the book was about. That's how we met the late Elmar Altvater for example, or our future colleagues on the stage. The way this research moves is similar to a spiral. Many times, you seem to be running around in circles, a lot of things don't amount to anything, and there are a lot of loose ends. But at the same time, this wide net creates a conceptual network that adds up to a clear mosaic, piece by piece. Parallel to this content-related research, there were a number of artistic, aesthetic decisions to be made. At some point, these two areas begin to overlap.

Daniel Cuonz:
I have a question about the concept of being overwhelmed. You drew us a picture of a heavily intellectual or epistemological challenge: *Wallenstein* or *Capital* of all things, books that are too long and to complex to fully grasp. But at first, wanting

to take *Capital* to the stage seems more overwhelming from an actor's perspective rather than intellectually.

Imanuel Schipper:
Let me take a step back to answer that question. Before we did *Wallenstein*, we did *Deadline*, which was about "ordinary death". That happened during a time when the so-called expert theater began, i.e. an approach that involved finding experts and installing their statements on stage. And I remember asking during a discussion: "Can you apply this method to a dramatic text, would that work?" That was a question of composition that we were interested in. *Wallenstein* as a production originated from that, and so did our concept of not taking a book's content to the stage, but rather creating a parallel universe of these works: constructing, composing a new world that mirrors the content, but works in a different way. We cared about that. And that's also how we proceeded with *Capital*. We realized that it would be complicated to adapt it for the stage. We based our approach on the biographical relationships our actors had with the book. We wanted to know about that moment in life when you hold Marx in your hands. What meaning does that book have for my life?

The path that took us there wasn't straightforward, though. Rather, it led past another production in Riga. There was an abandoned building, a former bank, which someone had re-staged for a theater festival. Over the years, this big, reverent building had served as headquarters for the *Wehrmacht* and the Russian secret service. Then it was part of the Riga city council, and now, it was completely empty – except for its lamps. The only thing they had found besides those was a box of files. And one of these files turned out to be a proposed screenplay for a *Capital* movie! *Rimini Protokoll* found the author and we learned that he had submitted the script for censorship approval in Soviet times, but never received a response. This man, this author, told the entire story of his never-produced screenplay during the play in Riga. That scene had the effect of a key moment later, for *Karl Marx: Das Kapital, Erster Band*. The biographic moment of a person with a book, that personal access, could be more important and more fascinating on stage than any production of Marx's *Capital* could ever be.

Jörg Metelmann:
You could break this story down to this: the theatrical invention when representing economics is that we need to analyze stories of trade among people. No abstraction, but specific trade with specific stories instead. We can come back to that in a minute. But I would like to continue with something else for now: the path from the

"everyday expert concept" all the way to *Hauptversammlung,* in which the entire reality was theatrically reframed and staged if you will. That's a long and important step, which made you famous after all. Can you tell us a little bit more about this transition from personal trade to re-staging?

Imanuel Schipper:
I think there were some connections already, at a time when I didn't even know the *Rimini Protokoll* people yet, when they were students in Gießen. And there was a project entitled *Bei wieviel Lux schalten Wurst und Schumacher das Licht ein?* about Frankfurt's energy supply. At the time, in the 1990s, city lights were still turned on manually. Two people were responsible for flicking the switch. The initiative, the theater project, was to go to this spot as a group, to get some interesting information and to attend that switch being turned on. At that point, the play was over, and you took a cab back to the theater. These projects are a kind of "ready-made", a performative *objet trouvé*. They're reminiscent of Duchamp's urinal. The idea is basically to reframe an everyday object in a special way, so that it becomes art. *Rimini Protokoll* developed a number of performances in an urban context. In these performances, the audience would assume a special position: in *Sonde Hannover,* for example, they would look down into the main shopping district from the tenth floor with binoculars. At the same time, they listened to an audio track. Some of it commented on what was going on below – which was unscripted. So, most of the performers didn't even know that they were performing. There are at least two lines of development that you can observe when looking at *Rimini Protokoll.* First, there is the production of plays that have a traditional, portable stage set. These are at the theater's disposal and people can act on them using all available resources. Besides that, there were site-specific performances that were harder to go on tour with.

When you think about economics and *Rimini Protokoll*, you could also start to think about how this collective managed to survive, for more than fifteen years, in a market that is shaped quite a lot by tendencies of change. They always asked themselves what constellation of theater formats is a good match for their portfolio. I think that's a substantial reason for their lasting success. In the last five years in particular, they developed formats like *100% Stadt* or *Remote X*. As a kind of sequence or series, these can be re-staged in different places. This way, there can be a guest performance while they can work on a new project in a different city at the same time.

Jörg Metelmann:
Rimini Protokoll didn't just survive, though. You became one of Europe's most important theater groups. How do you explain your success and the media's particular interest in something like *Hauptversammlung*?

Imanuel Schipper:
The often short-lived interest of the media can only be explained by conjecture. A lot of the time, you don't know whether there will be interest beforehand. In the summer of 2009, the project was a great match for the financial crisis, of course. But it's strange: there was only a small audience present for that production, 150 people perhaps, most of them journalists. But then there were six hundred "real" people attending the general meeting, and the business journalists or the *Tagesthemen* news team – which was there to report from Daimler's general meeting each time anyway. Another factor of this production was that this construct had a certain audacity to it – a "private" event is declared public theater. For one moment, a locked door was ajar. This revelation of a secret was attractive for a lot of people, adding a reframing of an event, which was dramaturgically clever in combination with picking Daimler as an icon for a German corporation. If you do a good public relations job, it will result in a certain attention.

Scott Loren:
Could this secret that you're talking about also be interpreted as the suggestion that there is something inherently threatening and unfamiliar to art?

Imanuel Schipper:
I think so. Or at least, it has that potential. It also resonated in our production about the World Economic Forum, *Weltzustand Davos*. This production played with the idea – or the fear – that someone, somewhere, is staging an entirely different, bigger and eerier theater besides the one that you can see. Many suspected that the WEF in Davos wasn't just a networking event, but rather that this is where the big global theater of power takes place. Organizers and journalists are partially responsible for this "paranoia" when they largely focus on whether or not *Rimini Protokoll* is trying to uncover a scandal. That's not *Rimini Protokoll*'s approach at all! We're much more interested in the general and dramatic structures of an event like that. In the case of *Weltzustand Davos*, the WEF understood that very quickly, and they were extremely supportive during our research. But still, there is always someone who thinks they know exactly what is being said. Some journalists

suspect a big scandal and start asking questions. So, there's always a wish for a potential danger present during a production like that for sure.

Daniel Cuonz:
There is a theater studies book on Ibsen's analytical drama that introduces the nice juxtaposition of "scandal value" and "fatal value".[1] Let's take *John Gabriel Borkman*. It's set after a giant scandal, a major scam. But when the play starts, all of that has already happened, ten years ago. Borkman has served his sentence, and we focus entirely on individuality. You could say that it's not about the scandal at all. Sure, that's a letdown, like hitting water. The fish move, but it's really not about the hit. It's about how the fish move. I'm sure *Rimini Protokoll* isn't all about the scandal value, but with economic topics in particular, it does play a certain role, right? And let me add: Perhaps the revelation of this secret, of this *arcanum*, isn't the kick in what you do. We're somehow aware that there's something going on in the background, and we'd like to finally see it. We want to understand it because it's very abstract. Abstract, but not hidden. That's your offer: the value of expression.

Imanuel Schipper:
I completely agree. When we did our research for *Karl Marx: Das Kapital, Erster Band* in Frankfurt, the topics of "stock companies" and "general meetings" came up again and again. And we asked several experts: "Can we join you sometime?" Every time, the answer was: "No, you can't." Eventually, we did get into Deutsche Bank using a by-proxies trick and with the help of a shareholder association. Of course, the setting was spectacular, but the content was boring and exhausting. All of the information is on the table, nobody says anything mysterious. But the tension, ours too, was gigantic. For me personally, the biggest surprise was Josef Ackermann. In this setting, in this staging, I thought he was the most convincing person imaginable. I would've entrusted him with my children, blindly, telling him that I trusted him. Staging trust, understanding and framing it so that it becomes visible: maybe that's the value of expression. It's a great match for the economic context, because eventually the economy and finances are always about trust. And so, *Hauptversammlung* has a double meaning: on the one hand, the content and the procedure of the meeting itself becomes visible for the audience, and with the help of the media, while, on the other, we can show that you can attend and observe this private and clandestine event under certain conditions.

1 | Matthias Strässner (1980): Analytisches Drama. Munich: Wilhelm Fink.

Jörg Metelmann:
Now would be a good time to get back to concrete issues, the procedures behind the numbers. We already mentioned this when we talked about *Karl Marx: Das Kapital, Erster Band*: visibility means seeing real trade.

Imanuel Schipper:
In such theater productions, trading happens on many levels. The first individual trade happens early on, during the research phase. Let's say you're interested in a certain Thomas Kuczynski, the last director of the *Institut für Wirtschaftsgeschichte der Akademie der Wissenschaften der DDR*, the GDR's academic department of economic history. You visit him in his apartment, and he's standing in front of a shelf that holds the thirty-five different editions of *Capital*, and he can tell you a story about each one. That's a successful trade. It continues in the rehearsal process: negotiations about the script, agreements, but also rehearsal times. These culminate in the performance itself: the audience buys a ticket, i.e., the promise to get to see a play. In *Karl Marx: Das Kapital, Erster Band*, there was another, special trade: in an analogy to the real *Capital* reading circles, there was something similar within the play. In one scene, we hand out copies of the book. Thomas Kuczynski has the audience turn to a certain page, and then he says "Ok, let's read this together now." Then, he comments on the paragraph. That would be a trade; "ticket price for comment on *Capital*".

Jörg Metelmann:
Let's talk about *Weltzustand Davos*, the play about the World Economic Forum that premiered in Zurich in January 2018. What was your approach, and how did it work?

Imanuel Schipper:
Weltzustand Davos was the last part of a tetralogy about post-democratic phenomena. We explored what was going on at the WEF in Davos in January, entirely phenomenologically at first. Is this really a meeting of an alternate world government, or is it just a well organized, elitist meeting of managers? Questioning that was the incentive for a big research trip that took us from the United States to China, to Geneva too, of course, and back to Davos and Zurich again and again. We couldn't figure out whether that was where the world's biggest decisions were made. But one thing was crystal-clear: if you want to make deals, it sure doesn't hurt to be part of the WEF. The former mayor of Davos compared it to the Diamond Club, a kind of special fan club of the local hockey team. You have to pay a lot to

get in, and there, in this Diamond Club, some deals that would perhaps be more complicated to realize otherwise are made directly.

We visited Davos right after the meeting, when it was dissembled. It was more than impressive to see how this event changes the city, how entire buildings are put up and brought down again, how another event space is added to every available area. And how billboards along the snowy main street advertise great investment opportunities in India or Mexico.

During the next step, we learned what an impressive institution the World Economic Forum is, what giant output it creates, what a large network of great people and important institutions it establishes. It's quite a fascinating overall performance that reaches far beyond the days of Davos.

Another aspect that we learned about during our research was particularly interesting for our topic of "post-democracy": states are no longer the (main) actors that solve certain problems in the world. In certain areas, private companies are taking on that job and, of course, they push approaches to solutions in certain directions. This force, which the agenda of a single company or a single CEO can develop, appears to be very strong and effective. The companies can push into this vacuum that can appear when democratic states, or states in general, can't agree, and these companies can act in a good or in a bad way.

Jörg Metelmann:
What kinds of ideas of expression did you develop from that? What did you, as people of the theater, do with these observations?

Imanuel Schipper:
For our series *Staat 1-4*, we had decided to give our relationship with our audience some special attention. We wanted to develop formats that involve the audience. We had discussed different kinds of formats for *Weltzustand Davos*, from a traditional on-stage monolog to a WEF simulation. We then agreed on a situation in which there would be expert actors and actresses, but which would also give the audience an opportunity to walk a mile in a CEO's shoes for a change. In the summer of 2017, at a Haniel Summer School - a cooperation between the University of St. Gallen and the Copenhagen Business School - we and a few business students had the opportunity to practice how you can assume the persona of a CEO, for example, and what information you need to do so. We also wondered if the audience could provide an image of those who attended the event in Davos. Accordingly, we made a statistically representative selection based on the last WEF's attendance list. We put the information the audience needed to play the

characters into individual books. Then, in some scenes, we asked the audience members to hold up a certain page. Those would contain a picture of a particular CEO, for example. Sometimes, we asked them for a decision as well: not their personal one, but the CEO's. That's probably the fascinating part of this production: that every member of the audience had to make a decision while assuming a role. The audience played the choir: the choir of WEF attendees.

Scott Loren:
I have a question about that choir in the *Davos* play. I feel like we talk about attention as capital a lot. If I understand you correctly, the choir gives attention by watching and perceiving. My question is: Can the choir fulfill its task if it only watches, only witnesses? Is this kind of attention sufficient to speak of a "choir"?

Imanuel Schipper:
I would even go a step further and not talk about attention, but rather about the concept of experience: the audience's experience. It always consists of an individual part, but also of a collective part. This experience, in turn, is the origin of the audience's potential reaction. That's the case for all kinds of theater, be they immersive, participative or what I call "relational" theater, i.e. all the kinds of theater that make it impossible to decide and plan everything out in advance because of audience participation. So, I would consider experience and the reactions to it sufficient to speak of an active choir.

Asking for experiences poses new questions to what one might call dramaturgy: How do you need to design the setting to make certain experiences possible? How does the economy of the rules of the game work? Should the audience assume functions as individuals or rather as a group or a partial group? *Rimini Protokoll* thinks it's important to produce as few opinions or attitudes as possible, enabling the audience to undergo their own experience, or several different ones. At the same time, an opinion that is too personal can lead the audience astray from the topic. The same question seems to matter for the WEF as well. We learned how fastidiously they choose the members of a panel and how closely they watch the preparations for contributions.

Daniel Cuonz:
In closing, I would like to ask you about the central term of the "expert". You made that one quite famous after all. There was a subversive component to it at the time as well. You announced experts – in our expertocracy, you can't survive without a commission that involves alleged expert knowledge – and then people got

someone with everyday experience. Let me apply this to the financial crisis. On the one hand, the general public has this need: that experts have to explain to us what happened. When you start looking for insiders, though, you run into a double-bind. Perhaps, these experts are even the ones who were involved in messing things up, and then they're asked to talk about the topic objectively. That's difficult. So, in that case, you have a juxtaposition of expert knowledge and being affected, or even guilty (perhaps just as an accessory). With that in mind, could you talk about your definition of "expert"?

Imanuel Schipper:
These experts are experts in their field, of course, in sociology or construction for example, but not in theater or on stage. What you see on stage are performers or staged experts. When we do our research, we visit "experts", of course, but in the rehearsal phase, they are performers. We work with them differently, because now, the actors in *Rimini Protokoll* are the experts for the on-stage adaption. We always make sure that they know that they are rehearsing for a theatrical process and not for a lecture or a construction site. The stage is an aesthetic space. The revolving stage moves as the expert reads his or her statement, and "Bonnie & Clyde" plays in the background. The entire scene is bathed in pink light. And still, the body that speaks is not that of an actor, but that of an expert. All things considered, his or her language is the language of an expert.

Jörg Metelmann:
Daniel also mentioned the pink light before: a re-framing that "shines a different light" on the expert and his or her knowledge, as you could say. And that's not so different from the strategy that Aeron Davis uses when he conducts his expert interviews with London bankers who tell him things they would never tell anyone else.

Daniel Cuonz, Scott Loren & Jörg Metelmann:
Thank you for a fascinating conversation!

English translation: Patrick Ploschnitzki[2]

2 | The translation has been reworked by Imanuel Schipper and the editors.

Productions Mentioned in the Interview

Bei wieviel Lux Schalten Wurst und Schumachter das Licht ein?
Theater project
By: Helgard Haug, Marcus Droß, Daniel Wetzel
Label: Ungunstraum
Production: Künstlerhaus Mousonturm, Stadtwerke Frankfurt am Main GmbH
Premiere: May 15th, 1998

Shooting Bourbaki – Ein Knabenschiessen
By: Helgard Haug, Stefan Kaegi, Daniel Wetzel
Production: Luzerner Theater, Expo.02
Co-production: Künstlerhaus Mousonturm/Frankfurt a.M., Neues Cinema/Hamburg, Sophiensæle/Berlin, BIT Teatergarasjen/Bergen, Avantgarden/Trondheim
Premiere: Luzerner Theater, January 24th, 2002
Winner of the 2002 Impulse Prize

Sonde Hannover – Ein Observationsstück
By: Helgard Haug, Stefan Kaegi, Daniel Wetzel
Idea / concept in collaboration with Bernd Ernst
Production: Theaterformen 2002
Premiere: Hanover, Kröpcke-Hochhaus, June 8th, 2002

Deadline – Ein Theaterstück über das Sterben
Concept / direction/ stage design: Helgard Haug, Stefan Kaegi, Daniel Wetzel
Production: Deutsches Schauspielhaus Hamburg (Neues Cinema)
Co-production: Schauspielhannover, Hebbel am Ufer Berlin, Burgtheater Wien
Premiere: Hamburg, Neues Cinema, April 24th, 2003

Wallenstein – Eine Dokumentarische Inszenierung
By: Helgard Haug, Daniel Wetzel
Production: 13. Internationalen Schillertage Mannheim, Nationaltheater Mannheim
Co-production: Deutsches Nationaltheater Weimar

Premiere: 13. Internationale Schillertage Mannheim, Probenzentrum Neckarau, June 5th, 2005
Invitation to Theatertreffen 2006, Berlin; Autorentheatertage Hamburg 2006; Züricher Festspiele 2006

Karl Marx: Das Kapital, Erster Band
By: Helgard Haug, Daniel Wetzel
Production: Schauspielhaus Düsseldorf
Co-production: Schauspielhaus Zürich, Schauspiel Frankfurt, Hebbel am Ufer Berlin
Premiere: Schauspielhaus Düsseldorf, November 4th, 2006
Awarded 2007 Mülheimer Dramatikerpreis

Hauptversammlung
By: Helgard Haug, Stefan Kaegi, Daniel Wetzel
Performed on: April 8th, 2009 ICC Berlin
A Rimini Apparat production in co-production with Hebbel Am Ufer Berlin, supported by the Acting Mayor of Berlin – Senatskanzlei – Kulturelle Angelegenheiten

Remote X
Concept, script, direction: Stefan Kaegi, Jörg Karrenbauer
Remote X is a Rimini Apparat production in co-production with HAU Hebbel am Ufer Berlin, Maria Matos Teatro Municipal and Goethe-Institut Portugal, Festival Theaterformen Hannover/Braunschweig, Festival d'Avignon, Zürcher Theater Spektakel, Kaserne Basel.
The production is supported by funds made available by the Hauptstadtkulturfonds Berlin and Schweizer Kulturstiftung Pro Helvetia. *Remote X* is created in co-production with House on Fire and with the support of the European Union Creative Europe Programme.

100% Berlin – Eine Statistische Kettenreaktion
By: Rimini Protokoll (Haug/Kaegi/Wetzel)
A Rimini Apparat production in co-production with HAU Berlin, supported with funds made available by the Hauptstadtkulturfonds.

Staat 1-4
Concept / text / direction: Helgard Kim Haug, Stefan Kaegi, Daniel Wetzel
Dramaturgy: Imanuel Schipper
2016-2018
The production series *Staat 1-4* is a cooperation of Haus der Kulturen der Welt, Münchner Kammerspiele, Düsseldorfer Schauspielhaus, Staatsschauspiel Dresden, Schauspielhaus Zürich, and Rimini Protokoll on the occasion of 100 Jahre Gegenwart. Supported by the Beauftragten der Bundesregierung für Kultur und Medien based on a decision by the Deutscher Bundestag. *Staat 1* was co-initiated by the Goethe-Institut.

Weltzustand Davos (Staat 4)
A Rimini Protokoll and Schauspielhaus Zürich production on the occasion of 100 Jahre Gegenwart
Concept, text, direction: Helgard Kim Haug, Stefan Kaegi,
Weltzustand Davos (Staat 4) is part of the production series *Staat 1-4*.
Premiere: January 2018, Schauspielhaus Zürich.

Networks Reworked

Interview with Paolo Cirio (New York)

Fig. 1: Open Society Structures – Algorithms Triptych, 2009. Serigraph print on Plexiglas. Courtesy the artist Paolo Cirio.

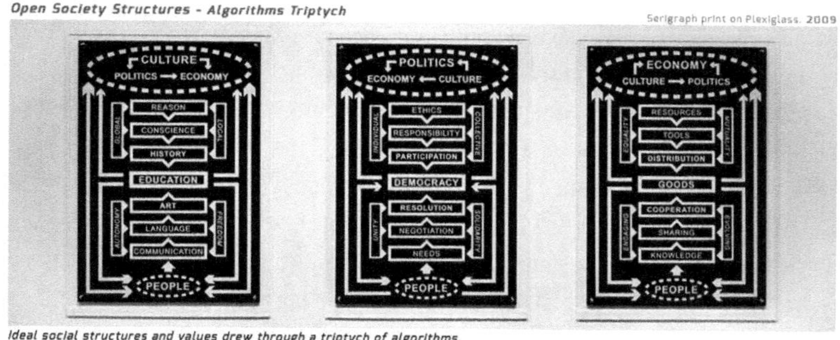

Scott Loren:

What are some distinguishing characteristics of your work? Is a signature identifiable in your choice and mobilization of medium, habits of aesthetic arrangement or recurrent conceptual politics of engagement?

Paolo Cirio:

I explore new modes of conceptualism, while also referring to early sociopolitical conceptual art. My work can also be very visual. Sometimes it even takes the form of photography. However, the works discussed here are deeply conceptual and visualized primarily with diagrams and flowcharts. I use these particular forms when my material is abstract and difficult to visualize with pictures or images. These works are characterized by flows of social processes activated by advanced information systems. With diagrams and flowcharts I can represent flows of information that would be difficult to visualize using other artistic media. However, flow in this context is not just about information flow, but also the social interactions generated across domains: social domains, economic domains, cultural domains and political domains often of global scale. As such I often talk about global information orders. How do you visualize global information orders considering that there is a particular power within that acts like it has agency and serves an agenda? For me, the best way to visualize such a thing is a diagram. A diagram can visualize the way I intervene and create in such an environment. That is how I came up with the artistic strategy of using diagrammatic language. The diagrams and flowcharts also refer to algorithms. A number of my works use algorithms to intervene in such systems. The diagrams are a form for visualizing and representing the abstract, quasi- or non-material elements relevant to this kind of art.

Things common to my art may be a kind of signature, but they are primarily things I care about. Most of my art functions and is communicated as intervention; and my work is usually informative. As active intervention, it tries to generate reactions. And while it tries to generate reactions in a provocative manner, it continues to be informative. The fact that my artwork will warn or inform the public about a specific issue they may be unaware of is a type of intervention. Intervention might be provocative to greater or lesser degrees, but if the work is informative, intervention is already achieved as far as I am concerned. What I care about, after all, is that my art is in the public's interest. For me, to make public art is to engage the general public or society as much as I can within my work. These are elements that characterize my work. Still, it is not easy to define my art in a sentence. And I do not like labels. They are very reductive. Using the label 'conceptual art' limits the discourse, as does the label 'intervention art'. Thus I would prefer to talk about a set of things that I use.

Scott Loren:
My intention was to get an impression of how you imagine your viewership as being able to recognize your work as patently yours.

Paolo Cirio:
Yes. But such categories or genres of art are limiting and thus counterproductive to me as a professional artist working with so many elements. Nowadays, an artist who wants to be successful might work in one medium with one style of visualization, using a logic like "For the rest of my career, I will only do blurred pictures so people can easily recognize my work and I can become famous." Art like mine takes a little longer to recognize. Maybe in 20 or 30 years my style will

be sufficiently present to make it recognizable. But it is difficult to be recognized now by presenting this kind of work, as its complexity requires various types of knowledge. It is not just about one thing, nor is what it is about achieved through one form.

Scott Loren:
Yes, still it seems this does not limit you from becoming recognized. Perhaps this is part of your appeal: aesthetic proliferation.

Paolo Cirio:
That makes it more interesting for the artist. Successful artists famous for one thing often become bored.

Scott Loren:
You claim elsewhere that digital information and communication technologies have "become the heart of the social order" (Cirio 2017). Can you elaborate on this statement with regard to economic presence and influence?

Paolo Cirio:
I think this clearly applies at the interdependency between information systems and social systems of today. What I generally call information systems includes many technological systems and accordingly has many names. Digital information may seem to have priority because the digital is the main mode of computation for networking diverse technological and social systems together. To me, though, it is a set of information and communication systems in total that we are concerned with. For instance, by communication systems, I also mean airports: any kind of system that enables the movement of informational objects through networks. As such, there are many overlapping networks of information systems interconnected with social systems.

Increasingly, connection is made on the basis of digital network technologies. However, considering technology at the center is reductive. If these systems and networks are interconnected, they can influence one another. Still, independent subsystems also exist: the subsystems of the airport, the subsystems of global trade. Then you have the subsystem of the law, the subsystem of finance, the subsystem of the media. With that, I mean mass media: they are still out there. There is the subsystem of culture, which sometimes enables the artist to have influence. All these systems are now interconnected through networks and thus mutually influence each other. I don't think there is a specific hierarchy. Some people say there is a stack. I don't know if you've heard of the theory of stacks, but I don't really believe this. Stack theory already takes for granted that there is a hierarchy: politics, technology, law. I don't think what we have is a vertical system. I think it's a network, and in a network each sub-network is able to influence other networks or even the entire system of networks. So when we talk about information and communication technology as the heart of society, it is a heart that is diffused in networks. My challenge as an artist is to address and engage these sub-systems as inclusively as possible; whether by abstracting the environment, making an intervention or by representing it. One of these systems is finance, the economy.

Fig. 2: (W)orld Currency, 2014. Two digital prints. Courtesy the artist Paolo Cirio.

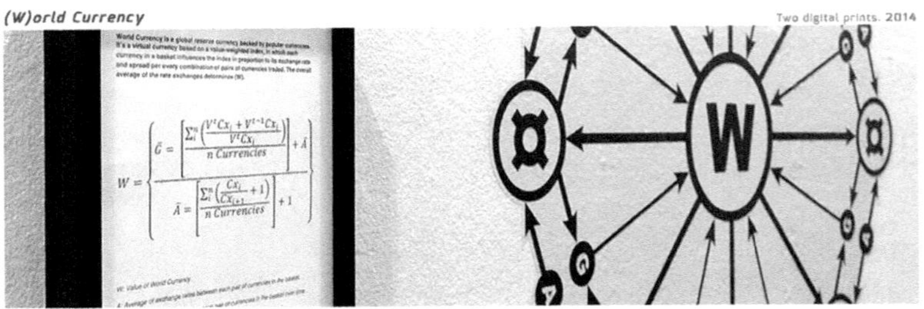

When you ask what the heart is, what the relation between technology, communication systems and finance is, we should recall in this context that finance started with the laying of submarine telegraphic cable between London and New York. That was the beginning of financial trading and the fact that traders could then exchange abstract financial instruments across borders. This was an unregulated communication system at the time, which facilitated the building of additional networks. Today, financial trading literally transpires through these kinds of communication networks. With trading transpiring through the Internet, they are not necessarily submarine telegraphic cables, but the systems are conjoined from the beginning. The communication networks involved also engage with the system of the law as with the system of the economy.

As such, I would make a distinction between economics, finance and the law. In the distinction between economics and finance, finance consists of these real-life communication systems where abstract financial instruments and products can be exchanged. This is now, our present moment, and yet finance has its roots in an industrial era economy. The history of economy is one in which there is a passage from late-agrarian and early-industrial human labor, consisting to a large degree in material fabrication and processes where people made things, to a post-industrial era in which machines started to make things. All that labor – and this is concrete economics – had to reorient itself and quite literally find a new job. In part, that job became the abstraction of finance.

Through my studies, I came to learn that it was politics, in the form of policy and laws, that allowed finance to grow, particularly in the UK and the US. The accumulation of capital in the industrial era eventually generated extremely wealthy industries as well as wealthy industrialists. At the same time, it also generated unemployment as machines occupied the factory floor and performed the work. And again, at the same time, laws were made to enable the expansion of the banking sector. Here we have a shift from economics, or economics proper, to finance and finance economics, thus initiating the post-industrial from within the industrial era. To talk about the post-industrial, though, we also need to talk about the post-colonial. Post-colonialism is very important for considering the space of finance, or finance from a spatial perspective. Finance is also a spatial communication system. The moment of post-colonialism is the moment when colonial power, which is economic power, had to be relinquished. The UK, the major colonial powers in Europe and the US as well all had to give up the two-fold power of colonialism. Colonized peoples would no longer be subject to cheap labor or slavery in the same manner. They would be granted independence. In theory, this is a granting of economic independence. In practice, however, sovereignty is withheld through finance: in the turn from economics to finance, finance becomes an important means of extending control over any potential economic independence. We see this when we look at offshore banking.

Fig. 3: Loophole for All, 2013. Two video channels and digital prints, US letter size. Courtesy the artist Paolo Cirio.

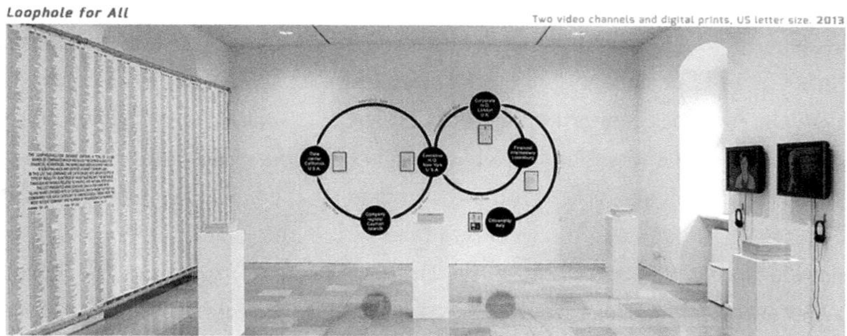

Consider spaces and centers of offshore banking, how the UK and the US have maintained and even strengthened communication infrastructures. We are still talking about submarine cables, but we could also talk about the construction of airports. In the post-colonial era, the UK built and expanded airports just as they expanded the banking industry, including the regulation of national and international banking law, in the same spaces: these are examples of interlinked and interacting networks of communication along which information carriers move. That is how we end up with international financial centers that are connected in diverse ways and which rely on a layer of laws determined by countries with colonialist histories. As such, the colonized spaces and the people who inhabit them are still subject to the will of wealthy colonialist nations. Colonialism still exists, even if its expression has become subtler.

Historical developments have enabled the connection of these three spheres – communication, economy and law – creating a joint political sphere at the heart of the social order. My answer, then, is yes: if we look at finance, information and communication systems are at the heart. And yet I would want to return to the notion that, with their respective matrices of sub-systems and sub-networks, these complex systems and networks are all interconnected. And the connections themselves are also of particular interest.

Daniel Cuonz:
You said something that I find extremely interesting. You claim that these systems constitute overlapping networks, and they define themselves in communication with each other. This is in perfect opposition to Luhmann's use of systems theory to describe social systems, where he claims that the systems do not communicate. Rather, the fact that they can be differentiated is dependent on their respective modes of discretion: a legal system alone has the functional procedures of a legal system, for example. And this feeds into Luhmann's qualification of modern societies in which hierarchy does not structure the relations of co-extant systems. Now, are we to assume that network society, with its complex of interconnected systems, produces a return to hierarchized social organization? The implication in such a scenario would be that where religion held the place of the hegemon in pre-modern societies, Silicon Valley holds this position in hypermodernity. Is it not the digital deities to the West that take on the role of key-holders, enabling the widespread internetworking of systems in communion? This would be Silicon Valley as a *passe-partout*. Does occupying this role constitute a system above the other systems, or would you frame it differently?

Paolo Cirio:

Of course, there are major players in these systems and subsystems. But to give you a counter-intuitive example, look at crypto-currencies. These currencies are not made by Silicon Valley. Sometimes it is just one coder who makes an algorithm that seizes control over networks: networks stretching from Wall Street to Silicon Valley to tiny European mountain villages. This is where we see the lack of a rigid hierarchy, where one small network or system, or even a single instantiation of agency, can suddenly influence all the others.

Staying with Silicon Valley, we can also take Twitter for example. Twitter controls the flow of information between millions of people worldwide. At least this is what they claim. But then you have Trump. Trump seizes a significant portion of control of that flow, and that impacts the entire system. He is not part of Silicon Valley either. He is able to mobilize a particular system to his own advantage. And he knows how to manipulate that system; a system that was designed to manipulate communication. Twitter is designed for the communication of just a few words. In this sense, Silicon Valley imposes on users the meaning of communication by setting the parameters of function. Then you have an unforeseen element, something like Trump, with its own communication strategies, which takes control over that channel and manipulates. Here we have an example of an individual who can take over a vast network and expand it beyond its conventional parameters. Now, what goes through Twitter with that kind of facility, if we stay with Trump, subsequently moves on to mass media. This is yet another network; through it he can amass and exercise control over (and through) vision worldwide. Trump's impact on flows of information through Twitter thus becomes highly visible to various groups even if they were not direct participants in the original system (Twitter). A further consequence of this non-hierarchical overlapping is that other politicians fall in line and begin using the same strategies. This is where we see hierarchies as diffused. Now everything is interconnected. One thing in one network can reverberate through the total network.

We are not really talking about anything special, to be honest. If we do in fact live in a network society, then theories of networks apply to our situation. We cannot apply nineteenth-century theories of the nation-state, with its notions of hierarchy and sovereignty. That mentality can be perceived in reference to a straight line, to the linear thinking of narrative discourse. It is no longer a straight line or a center that provides the point of reference, but the network. If this is the era of network society, I think we should look at society through theories of networks.

Scott Loren:
In "Aesthetics of Information Ethics," you suggest that a better understanding of the ways in which information technology constitutes social order can be achieved "through a constant reflexive examination of what it [information technology] produces in the social sphere" (Cirio 2017). How does your work facilitate this kind of reflection?

Paolo Cirio:
I would need to make a comparison to other kinds of work. This text is mainly about theories of ethics regarding representation and intervention in art, but applied to the medium of information systems. Again, we are talking about very abstract ideas. It is like material that is hard to see, or that is not even material in a way. It is diffused in flows and constantly changing, and there are so many subsystems involved. As such, some artists or academics will address financial systems in a very abstract or detached way, detached from reality in that they don't address what a specific financial system produces in a particular part of the world; maybe they fail to recognize a set of specific laws that allow a financial product to exist, or they don't address a particular group of people. Interesting graphs might be used and discussed in interesting ways, but we are still far from the real situational impact that produces the possibility of such graphs in the first place. At the end of the day, these networks impact the social sphere; and when I talk about the social sphere, I am talking about personal experiences such as how much one can afford to pay for rent or food as much as I am talking about the potential loss of democratic rights, or even the freedom to communicate with one another. These practical and intimately personal situations are ultimately affected by the same networks that provide the materials and setting for my work. My view is that when we talk about such complex systems – technological systems, legal systems – we also need to address the very personal side of things. We must be cautious in abstracting or speculating on them, as they have very important social and personal consequences. As such, to achieve reflexive examination in my work I directly engage with people affected or affecting financial systems, or I try to address the legal regulations that can influence the impact a concrete system has on some group of people who might eventually become marginalized or impoverished.

Fig. 4: Obscurity, 2016. Archival inkjet prints and mixed media. Courtesy the artist Paolo Cirio.

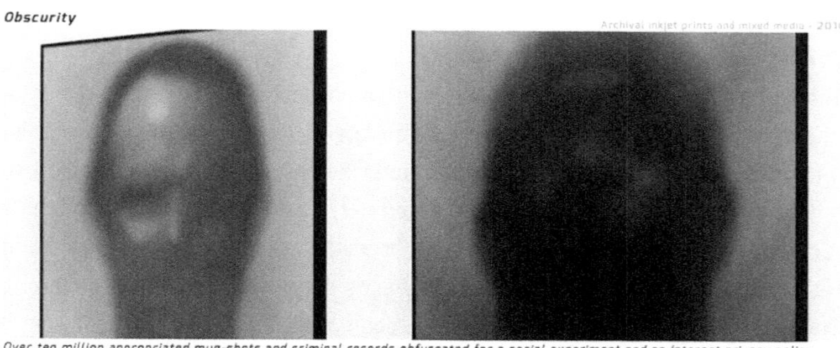

Scott Loren:
You make a distinction between "aesthetics of information ethics" and "ethics of representation and information systems", claiming that "representations of social and technological systems should engage with the dialectics of the construction of ethical value" (Cirio 2017). How would you specify your notions of *representation* and of *value* in this context?

Paolo Cirio:
First we need to make some distinctions. When it comes to the representation of information systems, the media (artists, academics and, in particular, journalists) tend to sensationalize and treat the systems as if they constituted a spectacle: a new power or environment. Elements like confusion, hype and fear are often used for this manner of address, or misconceptions might be applied to those systems. The ethics of representation is concerned with such issues: the way something is presented. Crypto-currencies are again a good example: they have been misrepresented by artists, the media and even by the financial system. We also want to distinguish between the ethics of information systems themselves and the aesthetics of ethics. The aesthetics of ethics is when you have social relations that the artist intervenes in or eventually produces. It is not something you can always visualize; it takes place across a dynamics of social relations that, in my case, is sometimes enacted through economic instruments and relations. The reactions generated – the interactions with audiences or institutions – are the real aesthetics: the relationships and interactions that constitute the aesthetics of ethics.

Scott Loren:
Is this the sight of or directly linked to representation?

Paolo Cirio:
Think about a painter. A painter has colors, a particular way of mixing the colors and of composing the picture. That is the aesthetic of the artist. Instead of colors and brushes as artistic tools, I have hundreds, sometimes thousands, sometimes millions of people, or bits of financial data related to institutions – proper banks, for example. I sometimes position them in a way where they can communicate with each other. Though in most of the cases they communicate to or through me. I might put them in an uncomfortable position or set of relations, allowing for greater or lesser degrees of control. These compositions of people (institutions, media, laws, cultures and economies), their interaction and reactions, are set up to create a particular kind of aesthetic. That is what I mean by an aesthetic of ethics. An aesthetic of ethics is usually relevant and present in performances. When performance art places the audience in an uncomfortable or unusual position, the reaction generated is that particular artist's aesthetics. In my case, the performances, the interactions and the reactions are channeled through information systems; they are on the Internet and expand to other channels. In the systems that I use, the actors are sometimes algorithms, and algorithms as actors have particular ways of functioning in the system: they are part of the ethics of information systems. And then you have the ethics of the work [of art] itself.

Scott Loren:
Where is value in such a dynamic?

Paolo Cirio:
Value is a concept I address in this text ["Aesthetics of Information Ethics"]. It is a matrix and is highly relative. I am convinced that value is about context. Context and the politics of context have becoming very central for me. Context gives meaning to what you do, as well as where and how you do it. Context has an enormous effect on value, of information as much as of an artistic act. If value is relative, it is context that makes the difference. We might expand on the idea of value in relation to ethics. For instance, moral values are contextual to cultures, opinions and environments; however, I refer to ethical value as universal principles. Let us take the value of a life, for example. Assume you have a context where you must have an opinion about killing someone. In this context, value doesn't really refer to your opinion. It refers to the actual subject of your opinion. You might

have an opinion, but if someone is going to die, you're not taking into account the element subject to the opinion, which is also the actual context that your opinion is ignoring.

Scott Loren:
So value is radically contingent on context.

Paolo Cirio:
Yes.

Scott Loren:
Your example brings us again to the element of participation, which is so important in your work.

Paolo Cirio:
Yes. We addressed this earlier with the notion that most of my art is done in the interest of the public, meaning a general public. However, the audience has become very dispersed and fragmented, especially from the perspective of art. We discussed network theory earlier. Networks do not turn everyone into an audience. Your audience is not a total-network mass of people. It may be in some regards, but it also consists of very small groups. Fragmentation into social bubbles is exponential. In these networks, Silicon Valley companies take advantage of fragmentation to target audiences. For my work as an artist, I am concerned with how to reach specific audiences, with having a language that speaks to a specific audience, or with placing the audience in a situation that is common for a larger cross-section of people. Of course, I design the work to get specific reactions. A work is successful when a particular audience replies with engagement, with any sort of interaction with my work. For instance, in reaching out to bankers I use technical business language, whereas for a general audience I use more common forms of expression or popular narratives to achieve specific types of interaction. So integration of the audience is pretty important.

Scott Loren:
This leads nicely to the next question, which concerns mimesis. You work with large recursive systems: digital information and communication technologies, social groups, institutions and infrastructures. As you so nicely put it earlier on, these constitute information systems and overlapping networks. Within these, there is on the one hand the audience component. A person encounters your work

and has a reaction. In perceiving and being in the presence of your work, one is also welcome to engage and becomes integrated into it. This constitutes one kind of recursion: the audience as integral to the aesthetic with the potential to generate a further audience that is also integrated into the aesthetic. On the other hand, there is the medial component: modes of distribution, medial contingencies and social contexts are present as central material and conceptual elements in your work. If we take the latter as the ethical dimension and the former as the aesthetics, to what extent do you draw on mimesis as a representational mode? Would you say that representations of dissemination, mediality and social impact in your artwork should subsequently activate reflection on that which the artwork critiques: flows of informational capital, for example, or recording patterns of individual behavior for repurposing as an economic resource? How much of what your work wants to critique does it also perform?

Paolo Cirio:
Not all of my works entail this kind of agency. Sometimes they are very conceptual. They are basically informative and seek to have an impact, but not all of them integrate agency. And sometimes they are agents with potential for agency in the framework given, but who do not act on the agency. When I run the algorithms, I call them performances, internet performances, for example. If we consider the nature of algorithms, the algorithm is an instrument that produces something; it is an agent. It processes information to make an outcome. The outcome is the agency producing the agenda, while the algorithm itself is the agent carrying the potential for agency inscribed in its agenda. Anyone who codes an algorithm has an agenda that gives the algorithm agency when it runs. You have the same situation when I intervene in these systems. Sometimes algorithms are schemes: legal schemes, economic schemes. True algorithms are codes. Due to the nature of true algorithms, which necessarily includes or adds agency, they produce similar kinds of reactions and outcomes. They impact the audiences we are talking about, or the systems that I target, or the institutions, and so forth. In this capacity, we can talk about representation and mimesis.

Fig. 5: Website homepage Loophole4All.com; Cayman 27, TV breaking news, Cayman, 2013; Royal Gazette, newspaper article, Bermuda 2013. Courtesy the artist Paolo Cirio.

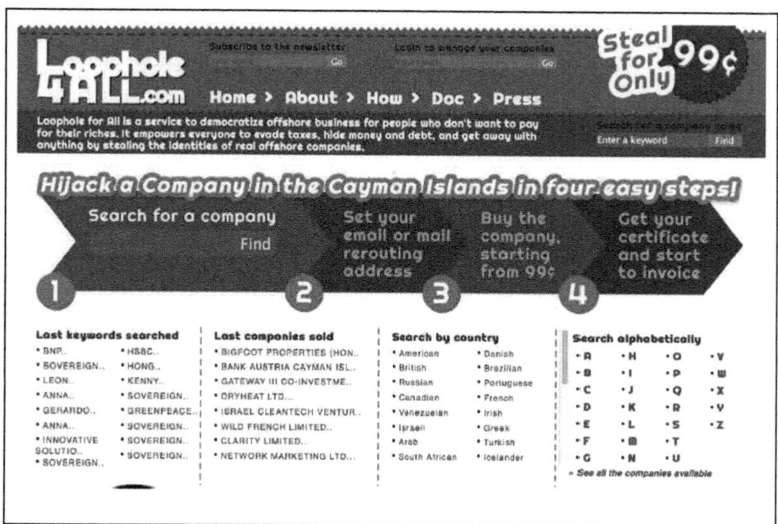

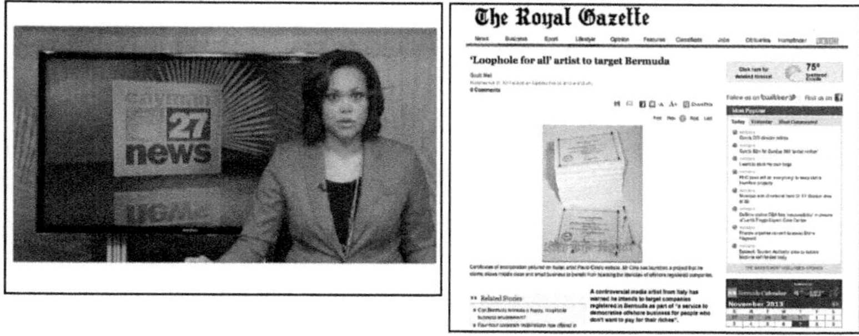

Scott Loren:
Could you say a bit more about the roles of the artist and the audience in this context?

Paolo Cirio:
This is a type of art, and art is usually considered a form of representation, of reality. With this particular type of art, which uses algorithms and networks - social networks, information networks - and where the material is the audience,

many hundreds of thousands of entities or individuals with agency, representation can produce very practical outcomes. Talking about change or changing the world is always a pretentious thing, but these works do have practical outcomes: in the artistic sense, in the social sense, in the informative sense. So here we can talk about representation, but with agency.

In my role as an artist, I sometimes take risks that can put me at the center of the networks and relationships in these interventions. This is also an articulation of the power and agency in these systems. This kind of embodiment also applies to the hacker: one single person in a bedroom messing around with an algorithm that eventually becomes a major crypto-currency, or that eventually generates large leaks of sensitive information. One individual takes that role of agency throughout the networks, potentially globally. That same embodiment, to have a contrary example, could be Trump. One person with his phone and with his stupid tweets takes risks by saying the things he says, but with the ability to affect the network throughout. Trump is also an artist, as the hacker is an artist. You might not imagine me in this type of role, but I do reenact these kinds of scenarios. My role as an artist can be one of enactment. Such a role of enactment in contemporary culture is novel if you consider that one individual in a bedroom can start a revolution or make a political coup. This used to require guns, thousands of people taking to the streets, taking over important buildings, for which you might need the military behind you. Now you just need a guy like Trump or Assange and you can affect the entire political environment.

Scott Loren:
Excellent. It may have taken some time for phenomena like these to materialize, but I think this is the potential that Hardt and Negri foresaw at the end of *Empire* – this kind of readily accessible bottom-up revolutionary potential inscribed into the digitally dispersive medium itself; or, to use your language, massive intervention made possible by the interlinked systems and subsystems of network society.

Fig. 6: Website homepage P2PGiftCredit.com; Paolo Cirio distributes P2P Gift Credit Cards in London, March 2011. Courtesy the artist Paolo Cirio.

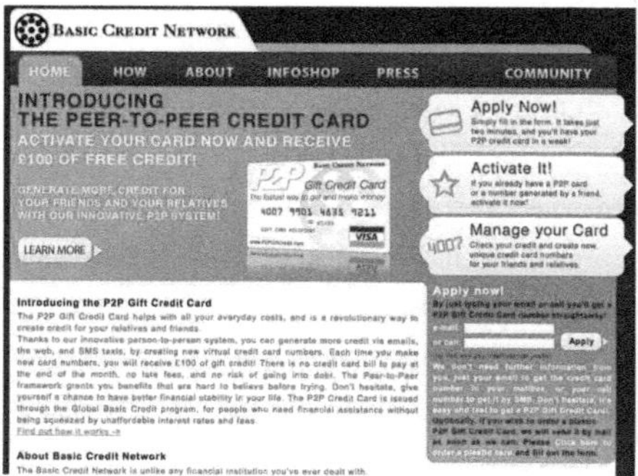

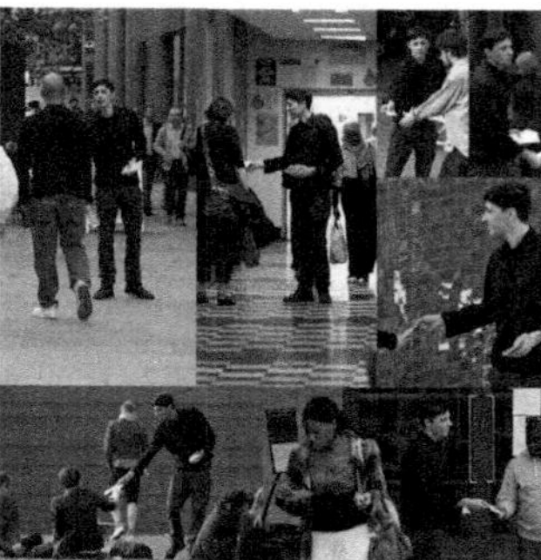

Scott Loren:

For this last part, we want to consider possible meanings of *the economic* and of *value* your work engages in or potentially perpetuates. These can encompass conventional categorizations of economy and value, such as the bank-issued credit represented in your *Basic Credit Network* (p2pgiftcredit.com), or less conventional ones, such as the negotiation of power relations through aesthetic and informational economies as in *Overexposed*, for example. Assuming there is something like a conventional perception of economic value present or identifiable in your work, what are its characteristics? What conceptual and aesthetic places does it occupy?

Paolo Cirio:

I don't know about economic value; but I do think there are cultural conventions in the economic understanding of society or conventions in the understanding of economic systems that I challenge or question with my art. There is a common form of intervention or aesthetic in my art that tries to break down financial conventions into economic systems; to break them down into smaller subsystems. We live in a complex world where it is very hard to see things or, regarding finance, very hard to understand things. In my aesthetic, when it becomes most informative, I try to break down complexity into smaller systems. Within those smaller systems I try to identify what is wrong with the flow, what the bug is, if you like. In accord with a hacker ethics, I try to fix or expose the bug.

Scott Loren:

The ideological dimensions of your work become legible when you describe critical art production and reception as ethical practices insofar as they are "ultimately oriented to maximize and develop the common good," and engage in "the making and understanding of a dignified existence for humans and the environment surrounding them" (Cirio 2017). By referring to and assuming a position in relation to specific notions of value in this statement – social value relative to community and responsibility, humanist values relative to individual rights, ecological value relative to perceptions of environment, cultural value relative to the contexts in which art might achieve particular impact – this statement itself already constitutes and contributes to an index for value. Your artwork explicitly participates in this type of value indexing when depicting intersections of digital media and economic praxes. But while your work engages in and incites reflection on critical points of intersection between economic praxes and information technologies, reducing it to a categorical dismantling (or rejection) of these would be a gross misreading. Why is that?

Paolo Cirio:

Let's assume there is some wonderful new operation system. It is great. Everyone should be using it. Perhaps everyone is using it. It is very powerful. But there are some problems. There are security issues that could potentially disrupt all of the user's work. The hacker steps in and says "OK, I've found the bug." By exposing it or fixing it, the hacker helps to maintain or improve the system. This attitude is present in much or most of my work. Even if the work is very conceptual, like *Open Society Structures* or *Global Direct*, there is a practical active attitude that says "OK, we can fix it. We can come up with better solutions, better systems, better algorithms." Even in the more conceptual projects that are highly interventional, like *P2P Gift Credit Cards*, the same is true. People subject to the credit card industry don't really question their actions. They get a credit card, run out of money, and amass huge amounts of debt, especially in the US and the UK, where the credit card industry is highly unregulated. It is very different in continental Europe, where there are stricter regulations enforced by law. And here we see where a simple law as a system can have a great impact beyond abstract representations of the notions of debt and credit. In *P2P Gift Credit Cards* the language is very simple at the beginning. "Look," I say, "This is free money. You can take it." This is the language the audience is accustomed to. I use the same marketing language as the credit card companies to capture the attention and interest of a particular audience. In this case, the victims of credit card companies.

They take the card, and when they try to activate it for use, they are informed about the financial model that victimizes them as well as about possible alternatives. The process thus simulates a situation of convention, and then confronts the audience with unconventional practices. And the conventions are culturally specific. For example, interest is prohibited in Islamic banks. In this context, interest is treated as usury and is unlawful. It might sound crazy, as this makes it a very different financial system, but for Muslim banks - which serve 40 to 50 percent of the world - interest is prohibited. It is a sin. If a Muslim bank lends you money, it will never take interest on the loan. It will demand a flat fee for the loan. This is just an example, but it might encourage us to question why we have interest-based loans as opposed to fee-based loans. Audiences participating in a project like *P2P Gift Credit Cards* will begin to have a better understanding of interest as a concept with specific conventions attached to it. They will come away knowing more about financial regulations and the deregulation of the credit card industry.

Now, we return to the question of finding the bugs and fixing the system. If we look at the last phase of this project, *Gift Finance* ends in monetary policy that the audience designs. In the diagram presented here you can see that although I retained basic control of the credit card - the treasury, the lending and borrowing - I designed the algorithm in a manner that would allow everyone to participate without being subject to the banking trade. Credit cards are a useful instrument, but they should be regulated and used in better ways. This type of system critique is very different from the nihilism or the postmodernism of critical art in the 1980s, for example. I am not saying we should be against the system *per se*. I am saying systems can be improved. And by the same token, I do not think trying to improve a particular system even constitutes an ideology. I think we can even leave out the question of progress. I wanted to return to the idea of being proactive here to give an example of an economic or financial systems and conventions in my work and the aesthetic place they might occupy. Here we see a larger system within which a problem can be identified and improved, and we also see the integration of audience, the role of the artist and the work's informative function. But in general, the improvement of a social or technological system shouldn't really have any ideological connotations. That is why I refer to recent aesthetic sensibilities in social practices art in the U.S. and in investigative art, as can be clearly seen in the essay "Evidentiary Realism." But I suppose it depends on what you mean by ideology. There are common goals throughout my work, but I am actually always against thinking of it in terms of an ideological dimension, even in terms of financial critique. I think this has been a problem.

Fig. 7: Gift Finance, 2010. Digital print. Courtesy the artist Paolo Cirio.

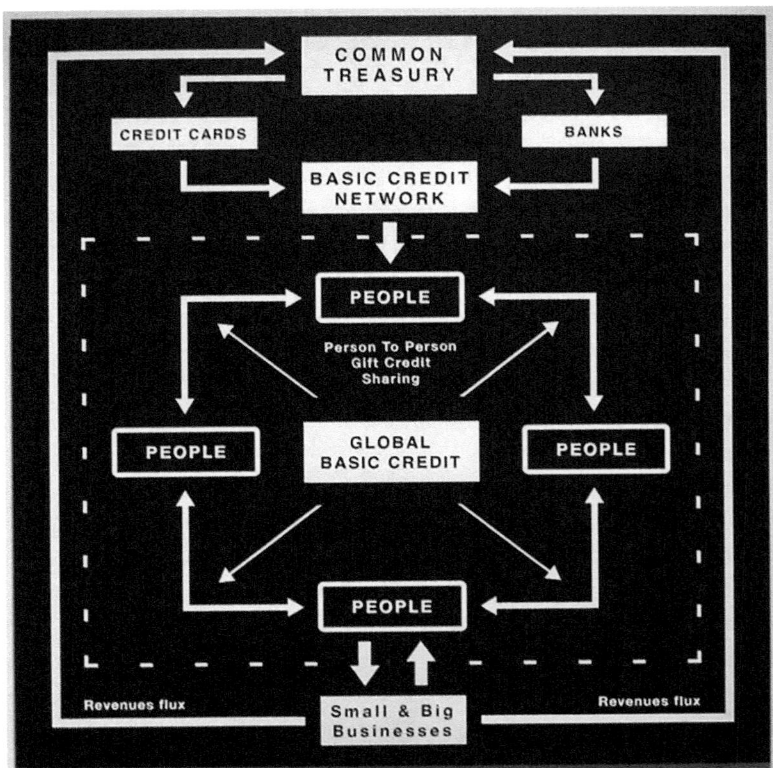

In the late 1960s, when we started to see signs of reinvigorated globalization in the expansion of the geo-political complex, artists began to explore the representation of its systemic intricacies critically and creatively. In the 1980s and 1990s we saw finance, centralized in London and Wall Street, become a prominent industry that affects world economies. At that time, artists and thinkers were not questioning what was happening. Finance was a kind of black box where money was being made. A lot of people were becoming rich. The fact that no one was really investigating it on its own terms played an important role. All of the theories and modes of analyses we applied to that world had actually come from or were designed to address the former industrial era. Marxism is the obvious example, but there are many others. This condition did not help us analyze and understand what was actually happening at the time. As a result, we have the dark age of the 1980s when Wall Street or the financial sector became very big and extremely influential. Then, in the early 2000s, the system collapsed. We have seen many crashes, but this was unique in the way it affected the West as a space of cultural value production.

That is why we are speaking now: that string of historical conditions generated a set of instruments to examine Wall Street and the financial sector, and to generate interest. Now, academics like you and artists like me scrutinize finance by breaking it down in order to better understand what is really taking place. My point is that if we talk about ideologies, no ideology could be sufficiently functional here. Ideology is too bound up in the past, not the present. You apply a set of preexisting understandings and values - they are preconceptions - to a system, but eventually they don't work. There is a mismatch between the preconceptions of ideology and the actual conditions of the present system. That is why I resist ideology. Some scholars, Marxist scholars for example, apply ideology or philosophy to examine the financial sector, but I think the ideological approach has seen its time and I don't think I use it. The means of production and intervention are now so diffuse and the playing field is so complex that the use of systems can turn out to be both for the good and be extremely dangerous as well. We might turn again to crypto-currency as an example: ideology would oversimplify the overall system. That is why I talk about ethics with regard to information systems and networks, but don't think ethics and human rights constitute an ideology as such. They are, rather, something more dynamic; contemporaries of our times.

Daniel Cuonz, Scott Loren & Jörg Metelmann:
Thank you for this fascinating conversation!

Works

Open Society Structures – Algorithms Triptych, 2009
Serigraph print on Plexiglas

Global Finance, 2010
P2P Gift Credit Cards. Digital print embossed plastic cards, dimensions variable
Gift Finance. Digital Print
Site: P2PGiftCredit.com

Loophole for All, 2013
Two video channels and digital prints, US letter size
Site: loophole4all.com

Daily Paywall, 2014
Newsprints and plastic newsrack
Site: dailypaywall.com

(W)orld Currency, 2014
Digital prints, document A4 and 100x100cm; Equation and algorithm

Obscurity, 2016
Archival inkjet prints and mixed media
Site: Right2Remove.us

Further Reading (All Texts Available at paolocirio.net)

Cirio, Paolo (2011-2014): Social Algorithm Art
Cirio, Paolo (2014): Text Project recap "*(W)orld Currency*"
Cirio, Paolo (2014): *Daily Paywall* essay
Cirio, Paolo (2016): *Obscurity* essay
Cirio, Paolo (2017): Aesthetics of Information Ethics

References

Hardt, Michael/Negri, Antonio (2000): *Empire.* Cambridge: Harvard University Press.
Luhmann, Niklas (1998): *Observations on Modernity.* Stanford: Stanford University Press.

Forget Neoliberalism: It's Financialization, Stupid!

Interview with Aeron Davis (London)

Daniel Cuonz:
In your recent work you argue that public debates on the economy (and on the reasons for the crisis of 2008 in particular) have been focused all too one-sidedly on the notion of neoliberalism. You say that much of what has been happening is better thought of as "financialization". Could you explain the difference between these two concepts?

Aeron Davis:
There are a whole set of differences. Part of the problem is that politicians, the public, critics and scholars have looked at free markets in neoliberalism and they put them all together with financialization. And although politicians implementing neoliberalism do not especially use this word – they use terms like "free markets", "free choice" or "*laisser faire*" – it is quite clear that they think that the old ways of managing the economy, such as state management, large unions and corporatism, are wrong, and so they tend to encourage market solutions and a reduction of state intervention in the national economy. That is partly about politics, partly about public rhetoric, and it's also about the critics of neoliberalism and what they focus on.

In contrast, although everyone looked to the financial sector as casting off the financial and wider economic crisis, there is less understanding of what financialization was doing generally before then. So perhaps there was a focus on the bubble and crash as a temporary effect, but in terms of the way economies have been managed in the larger scope of things, the big story of the past 30 years behind the neoliberal discourse, be it from critics or advocates, was the huge growth of finance. Just to give you an example from Britain, the financial assets managed by the banking community were something approximating half of GDP (gross domestic product) for half a century. From the 1980s onwards, there was a massive expansion until we got to the crash, when the assets managed by the financial sector were ten times GDP. When I first looked at the UK Stock Market at the end of the 1970s, the value of the FTSE 100 was a fraction of government expenditure. By the time it came to the crash, it was three and a half times the value of government expenditure. So the amount of assets the financial sector was managing, in banks and stock markets, all hugely expanded. The way finance was managed was being transferred more and more into big international investors' hands.

So all politicians were talking about the real economy, and jobs and employment and manufacturing, but in the background the real change was that capital was invisibly finding its way into the financial sector. Even after the crash there was a continuing focus on economic instability, on things like the very rich, on inequality, on restoring manufacturing and those sorts of things. So many critics continued to focus on neoliberalism rather than the technicalities of what had happened in terms of the real economy – the real economy being sucked up in many ways and put under the influence of the international financial community.

There are many differences about how people envisage finance and financial markets *versus* ordinary product markets, and from my perspective, having interviewed many people in both worlds, there is quite a difference in how they perceive and think about markets. And that influence affects policy and regulation as well as the wider public discussion.

Daniel Cuonz:
I would like to know more about what you mean by "perception" in this particular context, all the more so because in your writings, this notion is often paralleled with the notion of representation. Could we say that the difference between neoliberalism and financialization is determined by how the economy is perceived and represented by those at the top?

Aeron Davis:
This is related to who is being reported about in the financial and economic and business media. When a government is talking about a budget or some new economic legislation, then there is a political debate, but that is very much in relation to the national economy: jobs, employment, taxes, whether individuals feel better or worse off, whether the British economy is in good shape or not.

But most of the time most of the content in the business news sections is more about day-to-day investment questions. These sources think about some of these macroeconomic indicators – growth, the value of the currency – but they are very much thinking of parts of the national economy as temporary investment sites. That might just be about a company or about a whole sector, the sector of supermarkets, for example, or the high-tech sector. So when they talk about it and represent it and think about it and, therefore, evaluate the strength of an economy, it often has to do with how they perceive the investment opportunity. Good examples are the FTSE 100 in Britain and the New York Stock Exchange. When there is a discussion in the national media to show that the economy is healthy, they show the FTSE or the New York Stock Exchange going up, as an indication that a national economy is doing well. Except, the FTSE 100 has very little to do the national economy anymore. Changes in share values often relate to what is going on in these disembedded financial markets. Most of the companies quoted are multinationals that make more money and employ more people elsewhere than in Great Britain. You have been able to see this since Brexit. Ever since Brexit happened, every time there is some bad news, the pound's value drops, but the value of the FTSE 100 goes up, because they book most of their profits in foreign currencies. So there is this bizarre representation of the economy doing better because the FTSE 100 is going better, without the realization that this is about investment and not about the strength of the economy.

And it is the same with GDP. This single figure is used to illustrate growth, but growth can be based on a few factors which often do not take account of real people's experience of the economy or huge regional variations. Inflation indicators are another example. They do not take account of housing costs, which in Britain have gone up over six per cent per year on average in the last forty years, but they are not included in the inflation figures. So the government is saying: We have low inflation, but for most of the population, the costs of living are going up, much higher than inflation. So all these indicators are false perceptions of the economy. And part of that has to do with the investors' view of the economy, their view of which parts of the economy are good sectors to invest in, not necessarily the economy experienced by the population.

Scott Loren:

I would like to come back once again to the two key notions of your argument. In the framing of what you said so far, there is this sense of the possibility of putting neoliberalism and financialization on equal grounds as terms, which makes sense to me. I am wondering, though, if financialization originally might be thought of as something like a subcategory of neoliberalism, like any other economic aspect influenced by the possibilities that neoliberalism or *laisser-faire* politics opens up.

Aeron Davis:
I don't want to make the mistake and say they are completely different things. Because of course there are huge overlaps. I think what you are getting at is the question: What is the relationship between the two exactly? And I am not sure anyone quite knows. Because in some respect you can say that neoliberalism paved the way for financialization. But you could also say that financialization facilitated neoliberalism in various other ways. You could say that they are intricately connected.

There are important differences, though, one being the invisible mechanics and one being the visible political debate. Some countries are declared neoliberal, but do not have big financial sectors, say Canada, New Zealand or Australia. And then there are also countries like Switzerland or Japan that are not neoliberal in their political system, but have quite large financial sectors. There is not a simple parallel relationship or connection. One has to think of them as intertwined, but also as having their own separate developments and drives, and in some cases, like America or the UK, financialization has really boomed and not been accounted for properly. But it hasn't done so everywhere, and I am not sure why that is.

Daniel Cuonz:
The question of "visibility" and "invisibility" that you brought up in this context leads us to the methodology of your work. You mainly present three ways of collecting evidence for what you refer to as the difference between neoliberalism and financialization: economic elite interviews, public representations and news content analysis. Can you say a few words about each of them, perhaps with specific regard to what they allow us to see and where their blind spots are?

Aeron Davis:
What I do is more qualitative and social as opposed to quantitative. You could show a lot of aspects of financialization using quantitative data sets – most financialization scholars do this. But I felt you could not see the depth and what was happening on another scale without using more social and qualitative sets of methods. You mentioned content analysis, media representation and interviews. I often go to demographics as well, trying to look at the professional biographies and personal characteristics and education of those involved, be it politicians

or financiers or industry CEOs. You can tell stuff around that, too. One can also, as other studies have done, look at business biographies, the business reporting world, the kinds of outputs and productions of trends that are there in terms of their professional education networks, and so on for example. I haven't really done much of that, but other people have.

In terms of my methods, I think that the qualitative approach, especially the interviews, help you to realize that you have the official world and the unofficial world of practices and beliefs. The official world of, say, finance is very different and it often presents the official doctrine of rational and efficient markets. It is only by talking to people that you realize they do not behave in that way, and if you ask them about their methods, their thinking, their day-to-day practices, it's all quite different.

The other thing you realize when you interview more people in different business sectors is the big differences that exist in the thinking and behaviours between a CEO of a large industrial company versus a CEO who works in banking versus a fund manager or an analyst. What they do and how they see their role and see their position in the economy can be quite different. When I first started looking at this twenty years ago, I put together the financial and business community as one and then eventually I realised that they were not the same thing. And the more I went into it, the more I could see how fragmented the business community is and how fragmented finance is, and how people operate in their own silos and their own specialities, and can then be creating risks or profits or debts of tens of billions, without knowing what the guys down the corridor in the same firm were doing.

So it becomes much more important in these anthropological or social studies to really see what is happening, and to see that a) there are huge differences across these different sectors with different mind-sets, but at the same time, b) to try and piece them all together and see how they individually lead to certain outcomes in aggregate. We should not simply put it all together under "neoliberalism" or "big finance". It is a much more complicated story. So that's why I think we need to try and use these methods to tease apart what's happening and to have a better diagnosis and, possibly, a better regulatory outcome in the future.

Daniel Cuonz:

Is "outcome" also something that is at stake in the context of your research into the media coverage of economic and financial matters? You have made the point that economic news has edged ever further away from discussing 'the real economy' as it is experienced by most people and has instead come to be defined in extremely elite and financialized terms. Could you explain what this means in terms of "outcome" or, in other words, what are the consequences of this shift in media coverage of the economy and business, for example with regard to how people perceive important political matters like Brexit?

Aeron Davis:
First of all, financial and business news was always dominated by certain elites. But reading some of the histories of British and American business journalism as well as drawing on my own interviews, years ago, with people who were trying to describe how things were in the 1960s and 1970s and how they changed, I got a strong impression that economic news included trade unionists as they were considered very much part of the economy. You also had a lot of industrial relations reporters. These have virtually disappeared over the years. You had a lot more commentary from economists from university departments. You had more government figures talking about the economy and policy, not just being reported during a budget. But gradually things became more specialised and more dominated by the needs of financial markets. So in terms of generating the news in those sectors, financial public relations sourced the material. The media, while experiencing slow decline in recent decades, became more and more dependent on this output. And this output was focused on City economists and the discussion that was going on across the international investment community.

That misrepresented things. And it misrepresented the economic arguments around Brexit. I think that both sides got it wrong here. On the one hand, we had the "Leave" people who seemed to be economically illiterate to many people, who seemed to think that their Empire image of the economy would be restored and Europe was holding back our national economy. It is true that regions everywhere on Europe's outskirts do suffer under the European economic model. The closer you are to the centre the better you do, but if you are on the periphery anywhere, there is a problem. But, the Leavers totally failed to recognize that lots of other policies also caused the decline of the British economy. They completely misrepresented what the economy was about and where it was going. They were and are fantasists.

On the other hand, the Establishment, David Cameron, the City, the OECD, all these big high-profile economic institutions and so-called experts had been misdiagnosing what was going on for years as well. In many areas of the British economy, people had not seen their wages increase for twenty years, and they found themselves poorer in real terms, while being told that the economy was doing better. They could see that they were doing worse, that they could not afford housing costs and many other things that they used to be able to afford. Our employment figures showed record levels of employment, but what they did not show was a lot of what is now precarious. By the beginning of the Brexit year, 10% of the working population were employed in temporary, precarious and zero-hours-type contracts. And lot of the people who were working were still having to claim state benefits because their incomes were so small, even if they were working full time. And none of these things were there in the public debates. It was: "If we leave Europe, things will get really bad." And many people in large regions of Britain were being told that things were getting better anyway, but they were not. They did not believe those arguments. So why would they believe the experts saying it would be worse if Brexit happened?

So there was a misrepresentation from all sides of the economic situation, not to mention the fact that the British economy had been increasingly built on a series of Ponzi schemes in stock markets and finance and rising house prices. Basically, the British economy, like the US economy, was bust, but it was being covered over by the figures, by these other positive indicators. And all that was a misrepresentation.

Daniel Cuonz:
Do you think that some of the reasons for this "misrepresentation" can be expressed in terms of the *aesthetics* of representation? Financialization, you say, is still not sufficiently considered in public debate. Could this be because it easier to depict or to stage or to narrate the story of neoliberalism? And if so, would we not have to ask whether this is something that is actively instrumentalized by people who benefit from the process of financialization?

Aeron Davis:
Yes, that is correct. There is one larger problem, which is about representations of the economy in culture, in public discourse, and in the news media. If you look at surveys of what people watch the news for or read newspapers for, right down the bottom comes things like the economy or business news. There is no interest in that. People don't feel they have the knowledge to understand it. They will take an interest in, say, budget outcomes: Are they having to pay more or less tax, are they going to be better or worse off? And connected to that, most journalists are not that much more economically expert or financially literate than well-educated, numerate members of the public. So they struggle. The economy is a complicated subject, it takes lots of specialist knowledge, and it is fast-moving. There are huge amounts of data poured out in company reports and think tanks and gov-

ernment documents that your average journalist or your average person is trying to understand and just can't get a grip on. And journalists know that it's not easy to get viewers interested in the economy because it is not easy to represent – and finance is so much worse!

At least in coverage of the economy you can show people in a factory or on the streets or in economic activity, whereas in finance, well, you can show people on a trading floor, yelling and screaming (although they don't even do that anymore). Otherwise you can show figures and graphs. But that's not good storytelling. It does not get the viewers interested. And most people in finance, and certainly politicians, don't understand all the intricacies and complexities of many of the things they are dealing in. That came out after the financial crash. A lot of heads of big financial firms had no idea how their derivatives were working, let alone the cumulative risks. They just didn't understand them. I am not saying I understand them. I have a faint knowledge of a lot of these things, and I work hard and try to understand them, but probably 99% of the population, including a lot of journalists and people involved in the business world, don't understand the complexities – because they are highly technical and mathematical and are not easy to represent.

And, yes, in neoliberalism, critics can focus on figureheads, big corporate leaders who earn tens of millions of pounds or dollars a year. They can focus on these personalities. But finance is a different thing. I discovered recently, as I was writing something about FTSE 100 CEOs and their contribution to financialization, that these people didn't earn so much – well, they earn a few million a year, which is incredible by most people's standards, but when you look at the super-rich lists in Britain, there is hardly any FTSE 100 CEO or senior manager on there. Some of the people there are heads of private companies, but a lot of them make their money in other ways. Most of those are in finance. But the British media covering business and finance often interview FTSE 100 CEOs. We see them and we connect them to neoliberalism, and markets, and the national economy, but we don't see these other people whom most of us have never heard of. They are barely reported in the media. You can see a lot of the private company owners who are on the super-rich list. Some appear in the media. But if you do a search in the newspapers, they make comparatively few appearances. There is a strange misrecognition when you think of the British economy around government treasury officials and around captains of industry in the FTSE 100. But most of what is going on is other people, and they earn a lot more of the money, and they control investment, but they are not part of the media story.

There is also a problem with academics. Those who are not in business schools or economics departments (and even many who are) who are not interested in these questions. But if you talk to people who *are* interested in these questions, they are in politics departments or sociology departments, people like me who don't understand the real intricacies. We have a certain level of understanding, but not enough to really look at the details and say how to speak out. The critics of neoliberalism like Colin Crouch or David Harvey have rarely found their way into looking at financialization. They know it exists. But the neoliberal picture is there without finance having a big presence.

Daniel Cuonz:
What I find so interesting about your approach to these high-profile figures in the financial sector is that you don't ask the technical and probably much too complicated question "*What* they are doing?" or "*How* they became so rich?" but rather "*Who* are they?". So you are not trying to make visible what must remain invisible, but you shed light on what is all too often not taken into account in the investigation of the financial sector. In this sense, you write in one of your articles that further research on financialization – both in relation to neoliberalism and as an independent phenomenon – should include a focus on its "cultures" and "epistemologies". Could you briefly sketch out what you have in mind in this respect?

Aeron Davis:
There are two things: What I do is try and meet those high-profile figures on their place of work and ask them about their everyday lives, their practices, their connections, their social relations in their work lives. Increasingly, since the financial crisis, more and more people are looking at the super-rich, but they look at them in terms of their lives outside work, and I think that tells you a lot too, in terms of their dynamics and where they live and how they think. So there are two different sorts of approaches.

I am always fascinated when I get people's accounts of the super-rich and how they see and how they measure themselves. A super-rich person with only 2 billion dollars can still think of themselves as relatively poor next to the people they meet in Monaco who have fortunes of 20 billion dollars. It's relative. A company CEO or financier who has a bonus of 3 million pounds looks at the one down the road with a 50 million pound bonus. What I found in my everyday experience is just how mundane and ordinary a lot of this is. To these people, it's a virtual reality game. They're playing international investment inside their offices. They talk to other people in the same circle, but there are no ordinary people or industries or countries on the end of it. It's all very disconnected. But also their fears and their rationales are actually very ordinary. They are the same as those of ordinary people, although, again, they are represented as sort of better than ordinary; successful because they have this much money, more rational, more detached. But they have the same failings and failures and fears. Many of them are more likely to behave as a herd and to follow others, as a means of minimizing their own personal risk, as they are to be doing something new and different. And I found over the years that there are huge differences in what they do, but the products of their thinking and behaviours have a lot of ordinary similarities, which are very meaningful for the consequences of what they do.

One thing I have realized is the importance of mobility and precariousness. You usually think that precariousness has to do with the lower classes who can't hold on to a job, or migrants who have to move from one place to another to get work. But I have realized that the top tiers across finance and business are hugely mobile and hugely precarious. Most top CEOs in the UK stock market only have one-year contracts, renewed on the basis of their performance. A third of them do not last more than two years in the top position. If you try and survey financiers, that is impossible because no sooner do you have a list of top fund managers, six months down the line a quarter of them have left. They are so mobile! And discovering that sense of mobility and precariousness is important. On the one hand they are trying to achieve something but, on the other, they also know they are there for a very short time and then have to move on and disconnect from the company or the finances or the public. But it also means that they can maximize what they deliver to investors to gain their bonus, knowing it may do damage two years down the line. But that doesn't matter because they'll be gone by then. It's better to do that for one's own personal advancement than to make an investment in a long-term development. Because if you make a long-term investment, you still might get kicked out two or three years before this long-term development has become a great, best-selling product.

So if you interview enough of these people, you realize that mobility and precariousness influence their decisions and their strategies so much and they end up being bad for the business or the community. Their personal goals, their personal sense of risk is different from the risk of the company. That is the key factor. That is the kind of thing you only get when you trace these people, interviewing them close up and looking at their personal pathways.

Jörg Metelmann:
So one could say that on the one hand representation is a major issue when thinking about economic matters but that, on the other hand, we are often not aware of these types of misrepresentation that you are describing. One would think that the human factor is no longer important here, this is all digitalised, this is all flash trading, and these nanoseconds are unperceivable for us. But what is so interesting about your work is that it shows that the way humans set up their lives is of importance for the way they make their decisions and for how they do business. So we can take away from your work that we have to do more analysis of the misrepresentations of the economy, but also: "Don't' underestimate the human!"

Aeron Davis:
I agree. The great problem of the social science world, the journalism world, the policymaking world, is how they think and talk in terms of numbers and technology. They give the impression that they are real, powerful forces and you can't fight them, because they are like the sea. You can't fight the sea, just like you can't fight globalization or high-frequency trading. They dictate. But whenever you actually get inside and look, it is human beings making the algorithms, making the regulations, anticipating. And there are a lot of political choices. And yet we need to look at the human condition, the social and cultural aspect and not just throw up our hands and say: "Oh, it's too complicated! It's a thing we can do nothing about, that's the way of the world." Because whenever you challenge that mentality, people think that you are just a technophobe and out-dated. But we have to try and understand the technological and economic and financial changes, not just accept that they are an unstoppable force with no human influence there. That is what my interest in finance and neoliberalism is about: looking at power on a human level at the top and how it is much more to do with humans and social relations than many people would think.

Jörg Metelmann & Scott Loren:
Thank you for this fascinating and insightful conversation!

Further Reading

Davis, Aeron/Walsh, Catherine (2017): Distinguishing Financialization from Neoliberalism. *Theory, Culture & Society* 34, 27-51.

Davis, Aeron (2018): Defining Speculative Value in the Age of Financialized Capitalism. *Sociological Review* 66, 3-19.

Davis, Aeron (2018): *Reckless opportunists. Elites at the end of the Establishment*. Manchester: Manchester University Press.

Contributors

Marius Born (*1969) is a media professional with senior management experience in the TV industry. He is the founder of Born Media, and is currently advising Südwestrundfunk SWR in the repositioning of its TV sports formats. Marius was a member of the founding team of "ECO", Swiss public television's weekly business program, where he served as editor-in-chief from 2009 to 2012. In 2012 he was appointed Head of Documentaries at SRF, the Swiss public television company. His formats have won numerous awards. Marius holds an M.A. in Management & Organizational Psychology and he is a Ph.D. candidate in Argumentation Theory at the Università della Svizzera italiana (USI). He teaches at the University of St. Gallen and at Zurich University of Applied Sciences.

Paolo Cirio (*1979) works with legal, economic and semiotic systems of the information society. He investigates social fields impacted by the Internet, such as privacy, copyright, democracy and finance. His research and intervention-based works are disseminated through artifacts, photos, installations, videos and public art. Cirio's work has gained him international notoriety, garnering prestigious art awards, including the Golden Nica at Ars Electronica in Linz (2014) and second prize at the Transmediale in Berlin (2006), as well as an Eyebeam Fellowship (2012) and an NEA grant at ISCP in NYC (2017). He regularly holds public lectures and workshops at leading universities around the world.

Daniel Cuonz (*1975) teaches cultural studies at the University of St. Gallen. He received his Ph.D. from the University of Lausanne in 2005 and his Habilitation from the University of St.Gallen in 2013. His research interests lie in the fields of German literature, aesthetics, narratology and the relation between economics and literature. His latest book is *Die Spra-*

che des verschuldeten Menschen. Literarische Umgangsformen mit Schulden, Schuld und Schuldigkeit (Wilhelm Fink, 2018).

Aeron Davis (*1966) is Professor of Political Communication and Co-Director of the Political Economy Research Centre at Goldsmiths, University of London. His research moves between sociology, media and cultural studies, political economy and financialization. He is the author of six books and 50 other publications, the most recent of which are *Promotional Cultures* (2013, Polity), *Reckless Opportunists: Elites at the End of the Establishment* (MUP, 2018) and *Political Communication: A New Introduction for Crisis Times* (Polity, forthcoming, 2019).

Max Haiven (*1981) is a writer, teacher and organizer, and Canada Research Chair in Culture, Media and Social Justice at Lakehead University. His work focuses on the political economy and cultural politics of the imagination in several registers including the production of "imaginary wealth" under financialized capitalism, the radical imagination of social movements contesting it, and the way in which contemporary artists use money to open new horizons. His latest book is *Art After Money, Money After Art: Creative Strategies Against Financialization* (Pluto Press, 2018). He is co-director of the ReImagining Value Action Lab (RiVAL). More information can be found at maxhaiven.com.

Agustín Indaco (*1985) is a Ph.D. candidate in Economics at the Graduate Center, CUNY. His research interests lie in the intersection of applied microeconomics and big data and he is particularly interested in analyzing how to estimate economic activity using social media data. He serves as Visiting Faculty at the Strelka Institute, Moscow, and as a Research Fellow at the Cultural Analytics Lab (CUNY). He has published several articles, the most recent being "The Image of a Data City: Studying the Hyperlocal with Social Media" in *Architectural Design* (2017).

Andreas Langenohl (*1970) is Professor of Sociology with a focus on General Comparative Studies at Justus Liebig University Giessen, Germany. His research and teaching cover the areas of the sociology of financial markets, transnationalism and European Studies, social and cultural theory, and the epistemology of the social sciences and economics. Recent finance-related publications include "Modular sovereignty, security, and debt: The Excessive Deficit Procedure of the European Union" in *Finance & Society* (2017) and "Securities markets and political securitization: The case of the sovereign debt crisis in the Eurozone" in *Security Dialogue* (2017).

Scott Loren (*1971) teaches new media and cultural studies at the University of St.Gallen, where he was a post-doctoral researcher from 2015 to 2017. He received a Ph.D. from the University of Zurich in 2005. His areas of scholarship include film theory and history, genre and narrative studies, posthumanism and psychoanalysis. Interested in the aesthetic mediation of modernity, his current research is on technographic writing and technosocial transition. Since 2017 he is an adjunct lecturer at the Universities of Zurich and Berne, where he teaches expository filmmaking, composition and literary analysis.

Jörg Metelmann (*1970) is an Associate Professor of Culture and Media Studies at the University of St. Gallen. He received his Ph.D. from the University of Tübingen in 2003 and his Habilitation from the University of St.Gallen in 2014. His current research interests lie in the interaction between man and machine, the creativity complex and the future of business education. Recent publications in English include *The Creativity Complex. A Companion to Contemporary Culture* (editor, with Timon Beyes, transcript, 2018) and *Transformative Management Education. The Role of the Humanities and Social Sciences* (with Ulrike Landfester, Routledge, 2018).

Imanuel Schipper (*1970) holds a deputy professorship in Dramaturgy and Performance Studies at the Department for Arts and Social Change at the Medical School Hamburg. His research includes contemporary concepts of dramaturgy, performance studies and digital cultures, socially relevant functions of art and concepts of spectatorships. In his career as a dramaturge (theatre, dance and opera) he has collaborated with William Forsythe, Jérome Bel, Luk Perceval and others. He has worked with Rimini Protokoll on several productions since 2002, recently on *State 1-4*. Recent publications include *Rimini Protokoll: Staat 1-4: Phänomene der Postdemokratie* (Theater der Zeit, 2018) and *Performing the Digital. Performance Studies and Performances in Digital Cultures* (editor, with Timon Beyes and Martina Leeker, transcript, 2017).

Claudia Schnugg (*1983), is an independent researcher and curator at the intersection of art with science, technology and business, employing organizational perspectives, and cultural and social theories. She worked as Assistant Professor at the Johannes Kepler University, Linz, and was Visiting Researcher at CBS, the Art|Sci Center at UCLA and at ESO, Chile. She previously headed the Ars Electronica Residency Network. Recent publications include "Setting the Stage for Something New. Understanding Arts-Based Initiatives through the Lens of Liminality and Rites of Passage" in *Zeitschrift für Kulturmanagement* (forthcoming, 2018), and *Creating ArtScience Collaboration: Bringing Value to Organizations* (Palgrave Macmillan, forthcoming, 2019).